HEAD START

Also by Gordon Pape

Investment Advice
Building Wealth in the '90s
Low-Risk Investing in the '90s
Retiring Wealthy
Making Money in Mutual Funds
Gordon Pape's Buyer's Guide to Mutual Funds
Gordon Pape's Buyer's Guide to RRSPs
The Canadian Mortgage Book (with Bruce McDougall)

Consumer Advice
Gordon Pape's International Shopping Guide
(with Deborah Pape)

Non-Fiction
The Best of Pape's Notes
Montreal at the Crossroads
(with Donna Gabeline and Dane Lanken)

Humour
The $50,000 Stove Handle

Fiction (with Tony Aspler)
Chain Reaction
The Scorpion Sanction
The Music Wars

Also by Frank Jones

True Crime
Trail of Blood
Master and Maid
Murderous Women
Paid to Kill
Beyond Suspicion
Murderous Innocents

General
The Save Your Heart Wine Book
Come Home to Your Children (with Ayesha Jones)

HEAD START

How to Save for Your Children's or Grandchildren's Education

GORDON PAPE
& FRANK JONES

Stoddart

Copyright © 1998 by Gordon Pape Enterprises Ltd. and Frank Jones

Published in 1998 by Stoddart Publishing Co. Limited
34 Lesmill Road, Toronto, Canada M3B 2T6
180 Varick Street, 9th Floor, New York, New York 10014

Distributed in Canada by:
General Distribution Services Ltd.
352 Humber College Blvd., Toronto, Ontario M9W 7C3
Tel. (416) 213-1919   Fax (416) 213-1917
Email customer.service@ccmailgw.genpub.com

Distributed in the United States by:
General Distribution Services Inc.
85 River Rock Drive, Suite 202, Buffalo, New York 14207
Toll-free Tel. 1-800-805-1083   Toll-free Fax 1-800-481-6207
Email gdsinc@genpub.com

02 01 00 99 98 1 2 3 4 5

Canadian Cataloguing in Publication Data

Pape, Gordon, 1936–
Head start: how to save for your children's
or grandchildren's education

Includes index.
ISBN 0-7737-6010-5

1. College costs — Canada. 2. Tuition tax credits — Canada.
I. Jones, Frank, 1937– . II. Title.

LB2342.2.C3P36 1998   378.3'0971   C98-931480-4

Every effort has been made to ensure the accuracy and completeness
of the information contained in this book, but the authors and publisher
assume no responsibility for liabilities arising from its use. Readers
should use their own judgement and/or consult a financial expert for
specific applications to their individual situations.

Cover Design: Angel Guerra
Text Design: Kinetics Design & Illustration

See Gordon Pape's Web site: www.gordonpape.com

Printed and bound in Canada

To our grandchildren:
may their dreams
be affordable

Contents

Introduction

*T*here's no doubt that Canadian students are facing a crisis in higher education. It is serious now and it will be worse tomorrow. It is very unlikely that governments are going to reverse the trend towards forcing young people and their parents to bear the responsibility for an increasing portion of the university price tag. It's been said that we are moving in the direction of the United States when it comes to paying the cost of college. There's a lot of truth in that observation. The challenge in the coming years will be for individual families to respond. So far, they have not been doing a good job of it.

Education saving is not something that can be put off. Unless your family is very wealthy, or doesn't care if the children and grandchildren get a college education (in which case, why did you buy this book?), there is going to be a lot of careful planning and some financial sacrifice involved to ensure that the money is there when the time comes.

The sooner the process begins, the less burdensome it will be because of the magic of compounding. There are three steps to actually making it happen:

1. Everyone involved, but especially the parents, must make a firm commitment to do something besides worry about this issue.

2. Make a decision on what type of education savings plan is best suited to your family's needs.
3. Set up the appropriate mechanisms and actually start to put money towards the program on a regular basis.

Delaying can be very expensive. For example, let's say you have a new baby this year. If you put aside $2,000 a year for the next eighteen years and earn an average annual return of 8 percent, you will have accumulated a fund of about $75,000 at the end of the day (we'll leave taxes out of this equation, since you should be able to avoid them one way or another). That should be enough for your new pride and joy to complete a three-year university degree.

But if you delay starting for five years, you'll have to save $3,500 a year to end up with the same amount of money when the child reaches eighteen. If you wait until he or she is age ten, you'll need to invest more than $8,000 a year to make it happen.

As you can see, the longer you wait, the more difficult the task becomes and the less likely it is that you'll have the financial resources required.

This book is intended to clarify the problem, to show you the best and easiest ways to get a family education program on the rails, and to explain how to groom your child for scholarship success.

Be warned, however, that the process isn't as easy as we'd like. Unlike retirement savings, where the RRSP is clearly the vehicle of choice, there isn't a one-size-fits-all option for an education program. The federal government has created the registered education savings plan (RESP) and has recently improved the terms of the program as demands for more government aid have increased. But it is flawed in some important ways, and still represents a form of education roulette that could cost a family dearly in the wrong circumstances.

There are other alternatives, although they all involve trying to circumvent the tax laws in one way or another. For example, you can set up an education trust for your children, either formal or informal. In some ways, that's a more flexible and more attractive option, but trusts are not without their own sets of problems, as you'll read. There are also some loopholes in the tax laws relating to income from specific sources that can be used in this situation.

We'll look at all the choices and we'll discuss some appropriate investment strategies to use. In the end, we're certain we'll be able to help you find the right answer for your needs. If you have the commitment, your children will be able to get that degree. We promise.

Gordon Pape
Frank Jones

Toronto, 1998

Chapter 1

The Class of 2020

*B*ach. It was definitely Bach. One of the cello concertos. They were her father's favourites. Romney Anderson-Quan allowed herself the luxury of lying with her eyes shut, listening for a moment to the sound filtering down from the third floor. Then, with a prickle of conscience, she pulled back the duvet and glanced at the pile of books stacked beside her computer. But for now, she suddenly realized, the books could wait.

Eagerly she drew back the curtains, blinking at the bright sunlight. Her mother was already in the garden, cutting roses that would decorate the table when her grandparents came back for lunch after the ceremony.

"Hi, Mom," she called down. "What's the forecast?"

"Hi, honey. Like this all day! Isn't that just perfect?"

An outdoor ceremony in June sounded great in theory, but right up to the night before they had been worrying that a downpour might make it an ordeal for Grampa and Grandma. Still, Romney knew that not even an earthquake would keep them away today.

After washing, pulling on shorts and a top, and brushing her dark hair, she sprinted up the stairs to her father's office.

"Morning, Pops. Going anywhere special today?"

Jeff Quan turned, smiling, from the computer screen he had been studying.

"How's my little pomegranate on her big day?" he inquired.

"Dad," she said, mock-severe, "don't you dare call me that in front of my friends today. I'll never speak to you again."

Her father touched a button in the arm of his chair. The figures on the screen disappeared, to be replaced by a silver-haired Yo-Yo Ma coaxing Bach's timeless notes from his Stradivarius. It was her father's unchanging routine — listening to music and getting his daily fix on Beijing On-line, the Internet news service that, since the disintegration of Chinese communism, had become a mainstay for anyone like Jeff who did business with the world's largest economy. "You never minded me calling you that when you were small," he said. "It made you laugh."

"It still makes me laugh," she said, putting her arms around his neck. "Only for private consumption, okay?

"The class of 2020! And your graduation day! How did it all happen so quickly?" he sighed. "And how did it happen at all?"

◆

The class of 2020! It seems so remote. Yet the class of 2020 is already here. True, you'll find them today perhaps being breast-fed by bold moms in public places, or else taking tottering first steps — and running to Mom or Dad to have them kiss their little hurts better. Today you will find them learning at the mom-and-tot drop-in centre or maybe gazing at Teletubbies on television.

But right now, their university fate is being decided.

Decisions being made — or not made — by millions of Canadian families in these waning years of the old century will determine: first, whether our kids will be able to afford to attend university in the second decade of the next century; and second, if they go, whether it will be the sort of enriching experience a university education can and should be.

At this time, the picture could hardly be more discouraging. In the last decade, governments in Canada have shifted a major portion of university costs onto students and their families. For the future, they promise more of the same.

Moreover, the evidence shows that families are not shouldering that extra cost. Some are unable, some are unwilling, but the biggest reason by far is that Canadian parents have little awareness of the savings tools available to them to provide for their children's post-secondary education.

It is not their fault. In the past, schemes like registered education savings plans (RESPs) were badly flawed. Many people, including one of the co-authors of this book, put their hopes in these earlier savings vehicles — and were disappointed. Frank Jones had education savings plans for three of his six children. When none of the three went to university, he got back his principal, but the interest earned over the years was lost. The amount of money forfeited was considerable.

> **IT BEATS INFLATION**
> *While inflation in the Canadian economy has been beaten back to around one percent, education costs across Canada rose 9.2 percent in the last year. More increases are predicted.*

Although the plans have improved, they are still not well understood. Despite the overwhelming publicity surrounding the annual registered retirement savings plan (RRSP) bonanza every January and February, scant attention is paid to that second, equally important, family financial goal: investing in our children's future.

Now that mission can no longer be ignored. Governments, by cutting back their support for universities, have made that inevitable. The cost of attending university today ranges from $7,185 a year in Quebec to $12,374 in Newfoundland. By 2015 — one year before our Romney Anderson-Quan enrols — it is predicted that first-year costs will be $34,000, and that the total cost for a four-year degree will be $148,000.

The choices faced by parents and grandparents of young children are stark. For many of those children, even though they may not be in kindergarten yet, university has already been ruled out because their families will not be able to help. Others, determined to attend, will emerge with a degree and, like some of today's students, a crippling load of debt.

The frustrating truth is that if they only knew what to do, millions of families could avoid those pitfalls by acting now. How to do so is the purpose of this book.

EAST COSTS MOST

Of all ten provinces, Newfoundland in 1998 had the highest tuition and overall university costs. The roll-call on total costs for a year at university:

Newfoundland, $12,374

Prince Edward Island, $10,507

Nova Scotia, $10,139

New Brunswick, $7,960

Quebec, $7,185

Ontario, $9,886

Manitoba, $8,186

Saskatchewan, $7,789

Alberta, $8,709

British Columbia, $8,645

Source: USC (University Scholarships of Canada) Education Savings Plans

We began our research with Lorna Marsden, former senator, university teacher, and current president of York University. She made herself available to us on short notice because, she explained, she's convinced of the need for a book that will clearly explain how parents can provide for their children's education.

We met her and the university's vice-president of enrolment and student services, Deborah Hobson, in the ninth-floor executive offices overlooking the suburban Toronto campus.

Both women had the same discomfiting message: Canadian parents must start thinking more like Americans. "It's probably true to say," said Marsden, "that we're moving away from the European model, where university is free, towards the American model, where you pay for your own health care and education. But Canadian families have never had to come to grips with this in the way they have in the U.S., where parents are thinking about paying for university from the moment the child is conceived."

In the U.S., said Hobson, who grew up in that country, "Middle-class parents expect to bankrupt themselves for their kids' education. In this country, there is a mentality that says, 'The state will provide.' But government is withdrawing support from universities, and what's missing is any sense on the part of the middle-class that they need to pay for their kids' education."

Marsden faults Canada's financial institutions for putting all the emphasis on saving for retirement, but providing parents with little help or encouragement in saving for their children. "I have a bevy of grand nieces and grand nephews who are in kindergarten and Grade One," she said. "I've asked their parents what they're doing for their post-secondary education. They are all young people and [are] struggling; they think about it, but they don't actually do anything about it.

"I went to my bank and said, 'What can I do?' and they said, 'Not very much. You can have a savings account.' Oh, boy! I went to an insurance company, and they said, 'Well, you could buy an RESP, and if the kid doesn't go to university, you lose.' [The rules have recently been modified, but you could still lose under certain circumstances.] Nobody is making it easy. And the universities are saying, 'Oh, my gosh, we're the people who are going to have to do this, and we're not prepared either.'"

> **COMPUTERS COST MONEY**
>
> *You hear many complaints about the rising cost of textbooks. However, the biggest items on a student's supply list, according to the Canadian Federation of Students (CFS), are computers and software — now essential in many courses and universities. The CFS estimates that students' yearly computer costs are $3,000, while textbook costs are $850.*

Both women are worried that the new financial constraints will prevent the children of immigrants and the poor from attending university. "The lower you are on the socio-economic scale," said Hobson, "the more reluctant you are to take on debt, so again it confirms the pattern of the better-off going to university."

York, like a number of Canadian universities these days, is going out of its way to recruit immigrants and visible minorities. This is especially true, said Marsden, in nursing and teaching courses, where graduates will go on to become role models in their own communities. Again, an immigrant fear of debt works against these innovative moves. The result, according to Marsden? "The reinforcement of privilege."

They are concerned, too, that where parents and grandparents fail to come through with assistance, the lives of students will increasingly become a scramble for funds, taking away from the quality of the education. "We just had a reception for our circle of scholars with ninety averages," said Hobson. "Most of them don't have jobs while they're at school because they realize work is a liability if you want to keep up your marks."

University, Marsden believes, is about more than attending classes and doing papers. "If, the moment your class is over, you have to take the subway and go to your job, you're not taking advantage of what is here. People say, 'Oh, she can live at home.' But why come to university if you are not part of the team? Who plays on the team? Who is in the drama groups? We have students with marks in the seventies and eighties who are holding down two jobs. It's taking them years to get through, and they get discouraged and drop out."

Post-secondary education, too, she says, should present the chance to travel. Her university has a "third-year away" program, where students work and study in Guatemala. "Education is travel," she said. "It's working at a culture, not just going there for a week, but learning something about the realities. Is there any other time in your life when you can afford to sit and argue ideas, and not have to account for them?"

The university experience, enjoyed to the full, is a transition into adulthood, she said, and it costs money.

But do travel and exploring far-out ideas really cut it when it comes to getting a job in the real world? You bet, say Marsden and Hobson. "One of the characteristics of the workplace today is flexibility," said the vice-president. "And what you get from a university education is adaptability."

The twenty-first century, said Marsden, has been described as "the century of the liberal arts." What you will need, she said, "is critical thinking, flexible thinking, an understanding of the roots of our culture."

Yet, said Hobson, "the thing that amazes me, looking at my colleagues, is that people who themselves have had the benefit of a university education still have the attitude that if their kids want to go to university, they'll have to pay for it themselves. Yet investing in the next generation — that's the very best use you can make of your money."

◆

Jeff Quan put his arm around Romney's shoulders as they headed downstairs. "What do they say? 'Education is wasted on the young.' I believe it." He smiled wryly. "I know I've always regretted never going to university."

"You've done all right, Dad. You found the money for me and Julian to go." Julian, Romney's younger brother, was just completing his first year in music at Leipzig.

"Wait a minute," her father said, holding up his hand. "You don't really have me to thank. That was your mother. And Grampa Quan."

◆

"Hi, Mr. Quan!"

"Rosie, you have a new T-shirt. *Ni-i-ce!* And I like your shoes, Ryan. Cool!"

"Thanks, Mr. Quan." The kids on their way to Marc Garneau Public School just took it for granted that nothing escaped the attention of Mr. Quan, the crossing guard at the corner. They would have been mildly disappointed if he had not remarked on a new baseball mitt or a fresh ribbon in a girl's hair.

"Look at my drawing, Mr. Quan," cried a kindergarten mite. "I'm taking it to my teacher."

"Great, Madison. I love it." He hesitated. "A witch?"

"Oh, Mr. Quan! It's my mom!"

"Sorry, sorry. It's beautiful." Henry Quan lived for these moments.

At first, when he and his wife, Mary, sold their variety store and retired, there was plenty for them to do. Every day they had looked after Romney and Julian while their parents were at work. When the kids started going to school, Mary and Henry were always there for them at lunch-time and again after school. The children had never known what it was to come home to an empty house.

> **THEY'RE RAISING THE BAR**
> *The percentage of Canadians over fifteen with degrees or other post-secondary qualifications increased from 29 percent in 1981 to 40 percent in 1996.*

Then the kids grew up and did not need them as much any more. Mary and Henry went swimming together every day, but a lot of the time Henry felt at loose ends. It was Jeff, with his business connections in China, who had suggested job number one.

Now Henry rose conscientiously at four-thirty every morning, taking care not to disturb Mary, tiptoed into his office, and turned on his computer. By seven he had touched base with his Asian Web sources, condensed their information, and dispatched it to a dozen large corporate offices, where executives would find his business summaries on their screens when they arrived for work.

But that job took only two or three hours a day. And he was not meeting people. So he came up with answer number two.

Mary thought it was a bit beneath his dignity when he told her he had applied for the crossing-guard job. "You've earned your rest," she told him.

"I need to get out. I'm rusting away," he insisted.

Now, by eight every morning, he had read the paper, had breakfast, and was in the hall putting on his Day-Glo vest, ready to go to work.

The day he had put on his vest and stood rather self-consciously holding up his orange paddle to hold back the traffic for the first time, he knew this was for him. He felt needed. Now he delighted in seeing every familiar little face each morning and afternoon, and was concerned when anyone was missing. He loved the jokes, the secrets they sometimes told him. It kept him young, he told himself.

"You keep your mind on what you're doing!" Mary had told him that morning, just as she always did. Every day he came home with stories to tell her of what this child had done or that one had said. "You keep an eye out for cars, and never mind making jokes," she said.

This morning he had to be especially careful because, inside, Henry's heart was singing. It was all he could do to keep from doing a little dance as he stepped into the road, holding up his paddle. His Romney, his beautiful granddaughter, was graduating. Moreover, he had played a part in making this happy day.

◆

"Which vase do you want, Mom?"

"The tall silver one," her mother called from the kitchen. "It's on top of the armoire."

"I've got it."

Her mother was at the sink stripping the lower leaves from the rose stems. Liz Anderson-Quan would be fifty next year and her husband thought she was more beautiful even than when he had first met her. Her hair shimmered several shades of gold — part of her Norwegian inheritance — and if her face gave any clue to her age, it was in the laugh lines around her fiord-blue eyes.

"Darling, you'll have to get your new dress on. Grampa and Grandma will be here soon."

"There's time. Mom, do you remember your graduation day?"

"I'm not that old, darling. Of course I remember. It rained, but the show had to go on. I remember we all sat out there in the downpour. We had umbrellas, but what good were they! They all dripped down the necks of the people in front. I felt very soggy by the time my name was called."

"I bet that didn't spoil it, though!"

"Of course not. And anyway, I had other things to worry about."

"Like what?"

"I was going out with your dad by then, and we wanted to get married."

"Do you mean there was a problem because he was Chinese?" asked Romney.

"No, not that. Right from the start, Grandma and Grampa Quan treated me just like a daughter. I think they were shy when your father brought me home the first time — maybe we all felt a bit awkward."

"What about your parents?" Growing up, Romney had never seen herself as anything other than your average, normal kid. The Canada of the twenty-first century was a place where no one cared who your parents were. Plenty of her friends came from mixed backgrounds of one sort or another, and it had just never occurred to her before to ask.

"My parents? My dad was dead by then, but my mom — that was the big surprise. She really took to your father. She could not do enough for him. I think sometimes she thought he was too good for me," she said, laughing.

"Then what was the big deal about getting married?"

"The big deal was that I owed a pile of money. When I got out of university, the way I remember it, my student loans came to nearly $20,000. I know that sounds like chicken feed today, when some kids graduate owing more than $100,000, but then it was real money. If you were in medicine or law, at least you would be earning enough money after a while to pay off your loans. Architecture is different. Even when things are going well the pay is not great. But I graduated right into the recession of the early nineties. No one was building and a lot of architects were out of work."

Liz stood back and looked critically at the roses she was arranging in the vase. "I guess I never told you, but I seriously considered going into another line, maybe going back to school and taking engineering, something more practical."

"But you didn't."

"How could I? I already had that debt hanging over me. If I had gone back, I would have been middle-aged before I got out from under. The only answer was to get any sort of job I could. I went to business college and — well, you know the rest — I got to be a legal secretary, and ever since I've been saving Ralph Bragg's bacon for him at the law office."

"Mom, why didn't you go back to architecture when things picked up?"

Her mother waved her hand vaguely. "You know how these things are. You lose your contacts, you're not up with the newest trends. And then you and Julian came along and I was too busy to be launching a new career. However, it taught me one thing. I told myself that if you and your brother went to university, we'd try to make sure you got a clean start when you got out of school. It's not just going to university, it's what comes after. Thank goodness Grampa Quan got involved.

"Oh my," she said, flustered, "look at the clock, and there's the door. Darling," she called up the stairs as she passed through the hall, "I think your parents are here."

Mary and Henry stood grinning self-consciously on the doorstep in their Sunday best, Mary holding a bouquet of lilies.

Chapter 2

January 1998:
The Crisis Hits the Streets

Wisps of snow drifted by as Mary and Henry emerged from The Bay, Mary clutching the box containing the pink dress as if afraid the wind might snatch it from her.

"Here comes a streetcar," she said. "I'll see you back home." They had left her cousin Rose in charge of the shop, and she did not want to stay away too long. Henry had an appointment to see their lawyer in one of the shiny bank towers a few blocks away.

As he turned the corner, he was surprised to see police cars blocking Bay Street, diverting traffic. Not even buses were getting through. Must be a fire or something like that, he told himself.

It felt strange walking down the centre of the now-empty street, which was normally jammed with traffic. He could see no flashing lights of fire trucks, but as he walked on, he became aware of a distant swell of noise. He noticed a crowd jamming the street a few blocks ahead.

They were mostly young people, in their late teens and twenties, he would judge, and many were carrying placards that said Stop Student Debt. He wondered if he should turn back and come another day. But with those lawyers, the clock was always ticking where money was concerned.

"Excuse me, please," he said, coming to the fringes of the crowd, which now blocked his way to the silvery tower ahead. "Excuse me." People parted and made way for him, and soon he was in the thick of the throng. The noise was almost unbearable.

"Action — that's the only thing these people understand," bellowed an older, scrawny man with an English accent who was standing on the back of a white flatbed truck. "What we need is a general strike!"

Young faces were turned up to him. "General strike!" they chanted. "General strike!"

STUDENTS SHOULDER THE LOAD
From 1975 to 1985, tuition fees covered less than one-sixth of university operating expenses; by 1995, student fees, totalling $1.8 billion, covered nearly a quarter of university costs.
Source: *StatsCan*

◆

The demonstration that Henry blundered into on January 28, 1998, was part of a nationwide student protest. From Corner Brook to Vancouver, students took to the streets to express their long-simmering anger at fundamental changes being made to the way universities are funded. Throughout the nineties, Canada has been moving steadily away from the European model — where, for those qualified, a university tuition is free or nominal — towards the American model — where universities are, generally, for those who can afford them and where students are more commonly expected to pay their way.

The title of a 1997 Statistics Canada special report told the story: *Financing Universities: Why Are Students Paying More?* It revealed that student fees had covered 13 percent of university operating costs in 1980, but by 1995 that figure was 24.3 percent — and it's higher still today.

The most dramatic increases have come in the 1990s and have now reached a pace little short of breathtaking. In Canada as a whole, fees in the last two years went up more than 20 percent. The rate of increase varied from one province to another. In Alberta, it was 17 percent; in Ontario, 30 percent (with another 20 percent increase in store in the next two years); and in Newfoundland, 33 percent. In the twelve years leading up to 1989, while the cost of living increased by 38 percent, tuition costs jumped 155 percent. University administrators have little comfort to offer: "I expect tuition will rise significantly — and reasonably soon," said University of Toronto president Robert Prichard.

Why is it happening? Government grants to universities were already dropping in the eighties, but increased enrolment and modest tuition hikes allowed the institutions to bridge the gap. In the 1990s, however, it all came crashing down. Between 1990 and 1995, operating costs increased by 15 percent and deficit-fighting governments slashed grants. Where else were the universities to turn for extra cash but to tuition fees, which they boosted by 62 percent in that period.

All this happened at the very time students could least afford to pay more. Youth unemployment during the recession of the early nineties mounted alarmingly, while at home, family incomes were actually shrinking. From 1989 to 1994, the proportion of an average family's income needed to pay a student's fees rose by 58 percent — from 3.1 percent to 4.8 percent.

> **FAMILY INCOME FALLS BACK**
> *In the 1990s, tuition fees rose (by 52 percent between 1989 and 1994), but family incomes did not. Result: "By the mid-1990s, student fees were less affordable for an average family than at any time during the previous twenty years."*
> Source: *StatsCan*

Unable to earn the money for university themselves, and with their families less able to help them, students by the hundreds of thousands turned to the only source still available: loans.

Newspaper headlines in recent months tell of the outcome: "Repaying huge loans a barrier to education." And "The trap of rising student debt."

The Canada Student Loan Program was introduced in 1964 as a last resort for students. In the last decade, the percentage of students taking advantage of loans, both federal and provincial, doubled and, by 1998, amounted to 380,000 students — 60 percent of those enrolled. Debt had become a looming figure on campus, along with its inseparable companion, bankruptcy.

While 80 percent of borrowers pay off their loans without incident, in 1996 more than 53,000 were in default. The number declaring bankruptcy increased 700 percent in the decade up to 1996, when nearly 12,000 chose that option. The bad-loan situation became so dire in Nova Scotia in 1997 that the Canadian Imperial Bank of Commerce announced it was curtailing its provincial loan program in that province.

CANADA STUDENT LOAN PROGRAM BANKRUPTCY CLAIMS

Year	Recipients declaring bankruptcy
1990–91	3,300
1991–92	4,500
1992–93	4,500
1993–94	7,800
1994–95	7,000
1995–96	7,850
1996–97	11,800

Source: Human Resources Development Canada

Loans, which these days are made by financial institutions, are not simply handed out on request. Parents' and students' financial resources are examined, and the student can apply for a loan covering up to 60 percent of school costs. The maximum is $165 a day, which, with a top-up loan from your provincial government, brings the total to around $10,000. While students are attending school, their loans are interest-free. However, the interest clock starts to tick upon graduation, and the first payment is due six months later. For those unable to pay at that point, interest relief is available for up to thirty months.

While modest loans might have seemed a good idea in 1964, when university costs, even relatively speaking, were much lower, they have now become

FEES OUTPACE INFLATION

"Even allowing for inflation, tuition fees rose by 86 percent from 1983 to 1995. Furthermore, in each of these years, fees rose more rapidly than the overall Consumer Price Index."

Source: *StatsCan*

a millstone around the necks of thousands of young graduates. Statistics Canada estimates that the average amount owed by graduates has gone from $17,000 in 1995 to $25,000 in 1998.

With no end to the increases in sight, and the average cost of attending university at $12,690, students by early 1998 had had enough. They took to the streets.

"Right now, tuition fees are so high," declared Wayne Poirier, the Ontario chair of the CFS, "that they are an excessive barrier to post-secondary education. Many students are being turned away from pursuing a post-secondary education because they can't afford the costs."

What the student marchers were demanding from one end of the country to the other was a freeze on tuition fees. But away from the placards and the shouting, many Canadian parents with young children were addressing a disturbing question: If things are this bad for the current generation of students, what on earth will they be like fifteen or twenty years from now, when their own children are ready to enter colleges and universities?

And that led to a second question, one heard more and more at dinner parties, in chance meetings at shopping malls, or wherever parents encountered each other: How can I save now so my kid won't be in a bind when the time comes? One of the co-authors was even confronted by his doctor when he was in the hospital for an operation: How could he make the best provision for his son? he wanted to know. How old was the child? Seven months, the doctor replied.

◆

Pushing his way through the crowd, Henry found his progress suddenly blocked by a wall of students. Beyond he caught glimpses of a line of police officers pushing people back from the steps leading up to the bank tower. Suddenly an image of young people facing police, facing soldiers, came into his mind. He saw tanks, bodies. They were the images of Tiananmen Square. Images of the 1989 massacre, which never failed to upset him when he saw them on television. He shook his head. This was crazy. He was in Canada. Bad things did not happen here; this was a peaceful country.

Then a young woman with long, fair hair and wearing a knapsack lunged forward towards the police line. "No justice, no peace," she yelled in the face of a woman officer.

"No justice, no peace," the crowd chanted.

Suddenly Henry felt himself thrust forward. The pressure was irresistible. "Please, please," he pleaded, but no one listened. The police, faced with the choice of breaking or using their billy clubs, gave way and allowed the crowd through.

Henry felt himself carried forward as if he had lost the power in his legs. He was being pushed nearer and nearer to the plate-glass windows of the bank. He tried to dig in his heels, but that made it worse. He held the people behind him back for an instant, but then, like a cork shot from a bottle, he lurched towards the glass.

He glimpsed the frightened face of a young woman in business clothes behind the window. Then he felt and heard the crack of his head on the glass. He knew he must be falling, but held up by the crowd around him, he seemed to tumble in slow motion.

He was conscious of trampling feet, yells. "Back, back!" a male voice roared. "A guy's hurt." Henry tried to roll himself into a ball to avoid being trampled.

"Let me help you." It was a woman's voice. She was slipping her arm beneath his shoulders and trying to lift him. To his surprise, Henry noticed it was the young woman with the long, fair hair who had shouted a few moments earlier.

"We'll take him inside." It was an older man's voice. Still dizzy, Henry felt himself being lifted on either side. "You okay?" the man, who was wearing a grey suit and a conservative tie, asked him.

"Yeah, okay, I think," Henry faltered.

"You look shook up. You better come in and sit down. You want

> **CANADIAN SCHOOLS POORER**
>
> "In total, public universities in the U.S. are better off than they were two decades ago by the equivalent of $1,060 for each student enrolled. Canadian universities (due to government grant cut-backs) are worse off by $2,308 for each student enrolled."
>
> Source: University of Toronto provost's task force on tuition and student financial support, 1998

to hold that arm, young lady? I don't know how steady he is."

The woman with the long hair tucked her arm under his, and together they steered him towards the bank doors. Inside, Henry noticed that several hundred of the students, some still holding aloft placards, were seated on the floor in a corner of the huge banking hall while, behind the counters, tellers chatted nervously, glancing apprehensively at the interlopers.

"My name's Gordon," the man said. "I'm with the bank. Look, things are a bit dicey here. Why don't we take you downstairs to Second Cup for a coffee? Would that be okay?"

"Okay, okay," replied Henry.

"You too, Ms. . . . ? It's been an upsetting morning."

"Thanks," she said. "My name's Jennifer."

"You look as if you got a thump on the forehead," said Gordon as he brought over the coffees after they had settled themselves at a table in the concourse downstairs. "You feeling okay?"

"Yeah, I guess so," said Henry, touching with his fingers a small bump rising on his temple.

"You better call by at Emergency to make sure there's no damage."

"Maybe," replied Henry. "But it's in my stomach I feel bad. I never thought I'd see what I just saw upstairs."

"Exciting, wasn't it!" said Jennifer, smiling and stirring her cup.

"Exciting? No, no!" protested Henry. "This is wrong. This is Canada. This is a democracy. You don't need to march and shout and break in to places. This is a peaceful country." Henry felt a lump at the back of his throat. He was afraid tears might come.

"But look." She put down her cup, no longer smiling. "Sometimes there's no other way. You've got to fight and make a fuss because otherwise no one listens to you."

Henry shrugged. "But what's to be so angry about? We have a beautiful country; you can go to wonderful universities, maybe get good jobs. How come you're so angry?"

"Angry? You bet I am," she fired back. "Do you have any grandchildren?"

In all the drama of the demonstration, Henry had forgotten what made it such a special day. He looked down at his cup, a smile playing around his lips. "Yeah," he said proudly. "I've got a granddaughter. Born today."

"Then you should be out there shouting, too!" said Jennifer harshly.

"Me? Why me?"

"Because, Grandad, if things keep going the way they are, your granddaughter has about as much chance of going to university as she does of going to Mars."

"Now you're kidding me. If my granddaughter is smart enough, sure she'll go to university. Why not?"

Jennifer was rummaging in her knapsack. She pulled out a small bundle of papers. "Here, look at this."

"What is it? A bank statement?" The sheet bore the letterhead of the bank upstairs.

"My jail sentence, more like," she said bitterly. "See, read what it says. As of the end of December, I owed the bank $28,843.56. By the time I graduate in June, it will be higher than that."

"That's a lot of money," said Henry, "but when you start working, you can pay it off."

"That's a laugh," she replied. "I'm in the child-welfare field. Even if I get a job, with all the government pay freezes, it will be years before I am debt-free. But I'm one of the lucky ones."

"Lucky?"

"It's going to get a lot worse. Haven't you been reading the papers? Tuition fees are going through the roof. In the next two or three years, they are going to double or triple. Everything else is going up, too. Wanna know what it costs to go to university today?"

"What?"

"For four years, if you count lost income while you're in school, it comes to nearly $120,000. You want to guess what it is going to be when your granddaughter is ready to go? Three times as much? Ten times as much? Who can afford that?"

"But why are you making your big protest at the bank? Why not at the university, or maybe government offices?"

"Because, if you haven't already noticed, Grandad, it's the

banks that hold the real power in this country. It's the banks that hand out the student loans and make money off us, and it's the bank presidents who sit on all the university boards of governors. Right, Mr. . . . ?"

"Call me Gordon," said the banker, who had sat silent during Jennifer's harangue. "Well, certainly, some of our top people are on the boards. It would be odd if they were not. But in all honesty, Jennifer, we share a lot of the same concerns as you."

Henry looked at him with some amazement. "You don't mean you're glad they're marching outside your bank?"

"We're not nearly as upset as you might think," said Gordon. "We really don't want to see students incurring bigger and bigger debt loads. There have to be other answers."

"Wait a minute," said Henry, trying to take in this surprising shift. "You don't mean you're glad they took over your bank?"

"There are a lot worse things in this world, sir, than a few students sitting on the floor of the bank."

"You're telling me you're not going to have the police take them away?"

"You better believe it. Just picture it — footage on all the TV stations tonight of cops dragging students out of our premises and throwing them in paddy wagons. I can't think of anything worse for the image of the bank. No, sir, we don't work that way. We want to show solidarity with the students. After all, a lot of us who work here have sons and daughters attending university. We know what they're talking about."

The coffee cups had been empty for the last five minutes. Gordon looked at his watch. "I'm going to have our security people get you a cab at our expense to take you home or to the hospital, whichever you prefer," he said.

Henry, too, looked at his watch. "Oh, dear," he said. "I was supposed to be at the lawyers' office upstairs half an hour ago."

"Don't worry about that," said Gordon. "With all this going on downstairs, I'm sure your lawyer expected a few no-shows today. I'll order that cab."

Henry shook hands with Jennifer, and Gordon led him to

an entrance at the back of the building. He could still hear distant shouting as he got into his cab. What a strange place this Canada was, he thought to himself as he tugged on his seat belt, where a big bank would allow students to march in and occupy its property and its people would not even be upset. He had lived here so long, and yet there were still things he did not understand.

Chapter 3

University: What's It Worth to You?

"*H*igher, G'ma, higher!" The little girl's delighted shrieks rang through the playground, and Henry, pushing the new stroller with the big yellow wheels, stopped to watch.

"Steffany, that's enough!" cried a woman, obviously the girl's grandmother, steadying the swing before giving it another gentle push.

"Makes you feel young again, doesn't it?" Henry had not noticed the older man sitting on the park bench behind him. His attention until that moment had been wholly given to the exquisite peacefulness of Romney's tiny sleeping face framed by her white bonnet.

Spring had arrived early. The grass was already green by the first week of April, forsythia blossoms cascaded like falling sunbeams, and his daughter-in-law, Liz, had been only too happy to allow Henry to take Romney to the park.

"Young? Yes, it feels good," said Henry, raising his face to the sun.

"No, I mean watching the kids," said the other. "That's my little granddaughter on the swing," he added, with ill-concealed pride.

"You bring her here every day?" asked Henry.

"This is only the second time. It was my wife's idea. We get quite a charge out of it, as you can see."

"Yes, it's a lot of fun. This is my granddaughter, too. She's only just over two months old. It makes a big change in your life, right?"

"You bet. All of a sudden, everything else seems pretty insignificant. That's how we feel, anyway."

Insignificant. That described it exactly. Since the day Romney was born, Henry had felt distracted, disconnected. Mary had noticed. More than once she had had to pull him up for giving wrong change to a customer, and when one of their regulars inquired if his favourite cycling magazine had arrived, Henry had forgotten he'd put it under the counter for him that morning.

"Keep your mind on the job," Mary said sharply. "I don't know what's the matter with you."

Henry did not know either. You could say he was walking on air because they finally had the grandchild they had always hoped for. However, that was not really it. It was the encounter at the bank with the students that had upset him. When he left Mary the morning she had bought the dress for Romney, everything was as perfect as it could be. But as he rode home in the cab later, a small cloud had intruded on his happiness. Suddenly, Romney's future was not as assured as it had seemed earlier. He could not put his finger on it, but somehow he felt that he had a special responsibility where her future was concerned. Yet he really did not know what was expected of him.

EDUCATION MEANS JOBS
In the 1990s in Canada, 1.8 million jobs were created for those with post-secondary qualifications; for those without, one million jobs were lost.

"I tell you," the man on the bench was saying, "my wife and I, that's pretty much what we talk about these days. How Steffany is doing, the cute things she says. I know it's crazy, but we even talk about how she'll get to university someday."

"You talk about that?" said Henry, incredulous. "The little girl so small still?"

"Sure we do. Isn't that what every grandparent dreams about these days? I mean, Mr. . . . ?"

"Henry. Henry Quan."

"Henry, I'm Ben Czerwinski," he said, extending a hand. "I mean, we've lived long enough, haven't we, to know that education is the one thing that will make the difference for our grandchildren."

"You think so?"

"I darned well know it. I'm an economist by trade — retired now — but I keep an eye on these things, and they've been doing some interesting studies at the University of Toronto."

Henry pulled the stroller up to the bench, sat down, and turned eagerly to Ben. "You mean you can say how much it's worth to go to university?"

"Sure can. And as an investment, it's better than the stock market by a long shot."

◆

To read some newspaper headlines these days, you would think holding a degree or any other post-secondary qualification was a drawback. Articles about youth unemployment, while timely and important, have tended to focus, for effect, on graduates who have not found jobs.

Their stories, of course, have a special poignancy. These young people did everything their teachers and their parents told them they should do. They studied hard, went after a career, and now — zilch. And their fruitless search for work, or their tales of having to take jobs waitressing or pumping gas, make for sad reading.

However, the stories are misleading. Of course there are graduates without work, either through bad luck or because they lack the skills the workplace requires. But here is the truth: Without a degree or some other post-secondary qualification, your chances of getting a good job are low and getting lower all the time. And the corollary: a degree or post-secondary qualification is still the best ticket to a good job.

Figures from the 1996 census released by Statistics Canada in 1998 show that women especially benefit from higher education in terms of finding a place in the workforce. Of women aged twenty-five to thirty-four, only 59 percent of those with less than a high-school diploma were in the workforce. With a diploma, 74 percent were in the workforce, and the figure for women with a degree rose to 90 percent.

THE REAL COSTS OF SCHOOL

Tuition fees do not tell the whole story. The real costs of attending university are: tuition, 10 percent; food and shelter, 40 percent; forgone earnings (while you are at school), 50 percent.

There are still obviously jobs out there for men with fewer educational qualifications: 86 percent without a diploma were in the workforce. But of those with post-secondary qualifications, 97 percent were in the workforce. Conversely, the fewer your educational credits, the more likely you are to be unemployed. The unemployment rate in 1996 for those twenty-five to thirty-four with no high-school diploma was 18 percent; for those who had completed university, it was less than 5 percent.

As David Stager, a University of Toronto economics professor, puts it: "The biggest mistake that people make is saying they can't afford to go to university, or they can't afford to send their kids to university. The answer is, you can't afford not to."

Stager has been quantifying the benefits of post-secondary education for more than thirty years — for everything from Bible colleges to business schools. Simply by comparing the salaries earned by graduates in various fields with those earned by their contemporaries who have lower qualifications, he is able to put a figure on the value of a degree.

The table that follows makes clear that the rate of return varies depending on your field of study. And if that is the way you want to approach it, it allows you to pick the field where your degree packs the most punch.

The biggest surprise in Dr. Stager's calculations (which are based on Ontario figures, but are true generally for the country) is that, repeatedly, women derive more relative benefit from a degree than men do. Overall, a bachelor's degree gives male graduates about a 14 percent return, while female graduates score 18 percent.

It is not that women earn more than men do after graduating, only that they earn less than men do if they do not have a degree. Therefore, a female high-school graduate gets substantially less, for instance, than her male counterpart. With a degree, though, she is more likely not only to be in the workforce, but also to earn the same or close to the same salary as a male graduate. It means there is an even bigger incentive for women to go to university.

ANNUAL AFTER-TAX RATE OF RETURN FOR A UNIVERSITY EDUCATION

	Male	*Female*
Humanities, Fine Arts	7.3%	14.8%
Social Sciences	12.8	17.0
Commerce	16.2	21.8
Biological Sciences	6.8	15.0
Maths/Physical Sciences	15.1	21.2
Health Professions	14.9	21.0
Engineering	16.0	19.8
Law	15.0	16.0
Medicine	20.8	19.7
All Bachelor Degree Programs	13.8	17.6

Source: David Stager, University of Toronto

No wonder female enrolment has grown steadily — from one-third of the student population in 1970 to more than half today. In 1994, for instance, 60 percent of bachelor's degrees were awarded to women.

Stager's figures are based on the 1991 census. Therefore, it is natural to ask whether, with the dramatic rise in tuition fees in the nineties, the findings will still hold true when the 1996 census figures are analyzed. He believes so. In his original study, he found that even with a doubling of tuition fees, the rates of return would be reduced only by between 1.5 and 3 percentage points. It should also be noted that when you take into account lost wages while you are attending university, tuition fees still amount to only about 10 percent of the real cost of a degree. The odds also continue to be in favour of those with degrees because the wage gap between high-school and university graduates is getting wider all the time, and because the economy is doing well.

Stager has also looked at the factors that determine which

youngsters will go to university. And study after study, he says, show that the background and the attitude of the parents are the biggest factors. It is usually middle-class parents who went to university themselves who are most motivated to inspire their children to go after a degree.

There are, of course, exceptions. Canadian campuses today throng with students whose parents are first-generation immigrants who see a degree for their children as the passport to a life of prosperity and success in the new country.

Are higher tuition costs putting university beyond the reach of many?

The Canadian Federation of Students, arguing that tuition fees should be abolished, claims that they are not only keeping some away from university, but also are a reason others drop out. Enrolment at colleges and universities in fact continued to grow during the troubled nineties, although this may be accounted for partly by the increasing participation of women in post-secondary education.

Stager has tracked fees for most of this century and finds they have fluctuated significantly at different times. Interestingly, fees in real dollars were at the same level in the middle of the Great Depression of the 1930s, in the mid-1950s, and again in the late 1980s. In between, they've gone up and down (in real dollars) like a roller coaster. Over the last thirty years, up to 1997–98, arts and science tuition fees at Ontario universities rose by 36 percent — an increase of a modest one percent or so a year. Look at the shorter term, and a more dramatic picture emerges: fees in the last four years rose by 49 percent, surpassing the previous all-time peak in 1967.

That does not mean, though, that higher fees alone are making university expensive. Undergraduate fees, which average $3,100 and at the time of writing range from $1,663 in Quebec to $3,895 in Nova Scotia, usually make up less than a quarter of the out-of-pocket expenses of those attending university. Other costs include textbooks, transportation, food, and accommodation. If you also take into account lost earnings while you're attending school, the fees, as Stager points out, amount to only 10 percent of the total costs.

Textbooks alone, says Stager, have risen at a rate higher than the cost-of-living increase. "If I were forced to guess [which item would increase most in the future], I would say housing," he said. Students will either have to attend local universities so they can live at home, or they'll have to opt for institutions where housing is cheaper.

When their sons and daughters attend university in smaller cities, says Stager, some parents are buying rental properties. They can then install their child as manager and rent out most of the property to other students, a move that provides considerable tax advantages. (However, one of the co-authors did that when two of his children ended up at the University of Western Ontario at the same time and he was not thrilled with the experience. Being a landlord to a house full of students had more than its share of frustrations, and he and his wife were greatly relieved when the children graduated and they were able to get their money out of the property.)

Why, ultimately, are kids and their parents (and don't forget grandparents) prepared to put themselves through the financial wringer for the sake of that academic piece of paper? Of all places, we found the answer best expressed in a 1997 Statistics Canada education quarterly review entitled *Financing Universities: Why Are Students Paying More?* We think it's worth quoting in full:

"Broad access to university education is important because it offers more equitable opportunities for a better standard of living and sense of well-being. For example, university graduates are far more likely to be employed than their less-educated counterparts.

"Employment outcome differences are even more pronounced now because the costs of being less educated have risen markedly. Since the late 1970s, young people with only a high school education have had increasing difficulties in finding jobs, especially jobs that pay well.

"Even among persons who are employed, university graduates tend to have far higher earnings. They also enjoy higher levels of job satisfaction. For example, relative to their counterparts, university graduates have more autonomy at work and exercise more authority in their jobs.

"Over and above these advantages, university graduates are more likely to say that the greatest benefit they derive from their education is 'overall self-improvement.' Therefore, from several different perspectives, university graduates tend to be better off than those without university degrees."

◆

Romney had woken up. Henry leaned over the stroller, bringing his grinning face into her line of vision.

"Hi, sweetheart," he cooed. She gave him a gummy smile.

"My turn on swing duty," said Ben.

"G'ampa, higher!" dictated Steffany as she saw her grandfather approach.

The sun was almost summer-warm. Henry lifted Romney out of the stroller, perched her on his knee, and sang her a little song about a duck, which he remembered from his own childhood.

"Isn't she just gorgeous!" Henry beamed up at the woman who had been pushing the swing a moment earlier. "I saw you chatting with my husband, and I just had to come over and see the baby. What's her name?"

For the next fifteen minutes, they made grandchild talk until Ben, slightly red of face from his exertions, returned with Steffany holding his hand.

"I see you've met June," he said. "And I don't have to ask what you've been talking about. I was telling Mr. Quan how important it's going to be for these little ones to go to university someday," he told his wife.

"We've been thinking about Steffany's future already," said June. "I guess Ben told you."

"Yes," replied Henry. "But what if they don't want to go? You're always hearing about more and more kids dropping out of high school."

"I think it helps for them to know the money's there if they want to go," said Ben. "Our neighbour's daughter, whose parents have saved for her education, talks about 'my university fund.' There's no doubt in her mind that's where she's headed."

"So you think saving is a better idea than student loans?" said Henry.

"I never said that," answered Ben. "As an economist, I can see a role for loans. You borrow to buy a house, so why wouldn't you borrow to buy an education? Students and their parents should look on this like any other business proposition: how much will it cost, and how much can I afford to borrow? If a student is doing a part-time job, I'd tell them to quit the job and get a loan. The job may be paying ten dollars an hour, but after you graduate, you'll be earning twenty-five dollars an hour, and then you can pay back your loan."

"But you hear all the time about students who don't have the money to make the payments," argued Henry.

"Most of 'em," said Ben, "pay off their loans within two years of graduating. But I'd say students need more financial counselling so they understand debt better."

"So why save, Ben?" his wife asked.

"Because we're deeply irrational beings," said her husband, smiling. "In Australia, you know, they devised a scheme where students — or rather their parents — could pay their tuition fees up front and get a 15 percent reduction. A lot more than they expected paid up front, even though financially they were choosing the wrong option. Later they increased the discount to 25 percent to make it more worthwhile."

"Perhaps," said Henry thoughtfully, "they don't really measure it in money. Buying a university education is not like buying a car or a house."

"Exactly," said Ben. "We can talk all we like about the rate of return on a university education, but it goes way beyond that. Going to university has an intrinsic value. Otherwise, why do you see people eighty-five years old graduating? It's not because they're planning careers!"

Henry looked at him with a sly smile. "And what about when your granddaughter goes to university?"

June poked her husband in the side with her elbow. "Tell him, Ben. Tell him what we did."

The economist's cheeks flushed. "Us?" he said, a little flustered. "Well, the fact is we've just set up a growth mutual fund in Steffany's name, one that doesn't pay dividends, so the money will be available to her in capital gains when the time comes for . . ."

He was not allowed to finish his sentence. "G'ampa, teeter-totter, teeter-totter!" Steffany cried insistently.

"Coming, sweetheart. Coming," he said, getting up.

Chapter 4

Much Talk, Little Action

*H*enry took the mysterious telephone call at the store a few days later. The man on the line said his name was Steven Sniderman. He mentioned the name of his company, but with having to keep an eye on two kids over at the candy counter, Henry did not catch it.

"I have something of great importance to discuss with you, Mr. Quan," he said.

"I'm not in the market to buy anything," said Henry, ready to put the telephone down.

"No, no, I'm not selling anything," said the man. "Quite the contrary. It's an important business proposition I need to discuss with you and your wife."

Nothing to lose, Henry thought to himself. If the fellow turned out to be one of those two-bit hustlers, he would just tell him to get lost.

"We close up the store at eight tomorrow night, if you want to come around then," he said.

"Great. Will your wife be there at that time?"

The door opened just before closing time the following evening, and Henry caught a glimpse of a shiny black Mercedes parked at the curb. Sniderman was a stocky man, bald but with friendly brown eyes, and as he presented his business card, Henry recognized the red-and-black logo of a well-known real-estate chain.

"Give me a minute to close up, Mr. Sniderman," he said. "Then we'll go through to the back. My wife is in the kitchen."

After Sniderman left nearly two hours later, Mary and Henry talked until long past their usual bedtime. His proposition, if they accepted it, would mean a major disruption in their lives.

"We don't have to rush," said Mary finally. "Why don't we talk to the kids about it?"

This was why, on an overcast day, with rain spitting on the windshield, Henry was turning their ten-year-old Tercel into Liz and Jeff's driveway.

It took a while before they got around to the point of their visit. There was Romney to be admired, tea to be served, and talk of a hundred different matters before Henry could mention the visit they'd received from Sniderman.

"He seems a straightforward sort of man," said Henry. "He didn't try to rush us into anything. He said we'd probably want to talk it over and think about it for a while, and he'd get back to us."

"What kind of development are they planning on the site, Dad?" said Jeff.

"An office development, as I understand it. He said once they have all the block under option, they'll apply for a rezoning."

"Is it a good offer?"

"It sounds good," said Mary, "but that's not the point. If we sell the store, how will we live? Where will we get money?"

"Mom, if they give you enough for it, you'll have the money to live on. What kind of money are they talking?"

"Well." The older couple looked at each other and then Henry continued. "He said they might be able to go to $300,000."

Jeff whistled. "That's more than I ever thought the old place would be worth. And it sounds as if that's only the starting price."

"But where would you live?" said Liz, who was in the rocker holding Romney. "You'd need another place."

"I reckon we could get a nice little bungalow, one of those two-bedroom ones, for less than $200,000," said Henry.

"And what would you do with your time?" said his wife. "You're only fifty-five. You need to keep busy."

"Busy? I've been busy all my life," retorted Henry. "Now I want time to do the things I really want to do."

"Like what?"

"Like, well . . . well . . ." he spluttered. "Well, like taking Romney fishing!"

"She's a girl!"

"I know she's a girl. I'm not stupid," he fired back. "Girls fish, don't they?"

"Sure they do, Dad," said Liz, intervening to restore peace. "What do you think, Jeff, about your parents giving up the shop?"

"I think it's a great idea — if that's what you want," he said turning from one to the other. "Do you really want to spend the rest of your years getting up so early, working so late, tied to the business six days a week, fifty-two weeks of the year? You should have more time for yourselves. Time to travel. Haven't you talked about going back to Hong Kong for a trip, Mom?"

"But where's all the money going to come from?"

"We've got savings," said Henry. "We've been putting money into our RRSPs all these years. It's time we got some use out of it."

"Dad, why don't we go in the den?" said Jeff. "We'll do some figuring on the computer. My software will crunch the numbers for us and then you'll have a better idea of where you stand."

When they emerged half an hour later, Henry was beaming. "Looks like we can swing it," he told Mary. "If we're careful."

"I told Dad that you should both go and see a financial adviser when you have a better idea of how much money

> **PARENTS DUCK OUT**
> *In 1990–91, according to a detailed York University student survey, parents were the chief source of funding for students, with 57 percent kicking in their share. By 1994–95, when the survey was done again, student loans had taken over as the chief source, and now only 46 percent of parents contributed. A university official says he is hopeful future surveys will show parents increasing their aid once more.*

you'll have," Jeff told her. "There are so many angles to these things."

"We don't want our money to run out before we do," said Mary, somewhat mollified.

"No chance," said Henry. "As a matter of fact," he said, turning to Liz, "I could see us having enough money out of the shop to put aside a bit for Romney's education."

"Dad, she's only a baby!" Liz laughed. "There's plenty of time for that."

"No, no, you don't understand," said Henry. "I've been talking to people. There was this guy in the park. He's an economist, and he was telling me how important it's going to be for kids to have a university education. But the costs are going out of sight. By the time Romney is ready, you'll need a small fortune to go to university. You can't start too soon."

"Wait a minute," said Liz, rummaging under the coffee table. "There was something I saw in the paper only this morning. I meant to clip it out. Here it is."

She held up an advertisement consisting of nothing but a graphic headline: "In the year 2015, they say it will cost more than $67,000 for an undergraduate degree." At the foot of the page was the name of a mutual-fund company.

"Why I noticed it specially," said Liz, "is that a friend of mine just recently became marketing director at that firm. Her name is Christine Williams. I just met her downtown the other day. We were at school together years ago, but we recognized each other right away. She told me she and her husband have two little boys now."

"I bet they're thinking how they'll pay for university, too," said Henry.

"I know what I'll do," said Liz, making up her mind. "I'll give her a call, see if she's free for lunch. And why don't you come too, Dad? You'd probably think of a lot more questions to ask than me."

"You don't think I'd be in the way? Maybe you want to talk about when you were at school together."

"Dad, this is business," she said, giving her daughter a squeeze. "Romney's business."

◆

Henry had never actually taken a voyage on an ocean liner. Lately, though, since their encounter with Mr. Sniderman, the real-estate man, he had been hinting to Mary that if they sold the business, they might consider taking a cruise. But as he and Liz emerged on the forty-fifth floor of one of those downtown bank towers to keep their appointment with Christine Williams, Henry knew exactly where he was: he was on the bridge of one of the great liners.

The mutual-fund company's vast reception area was dominated by a curving canopy, just like the bridge of a ship, while the substantial navy blue furniture with white piping repeated the nautical theme. When a secretary arrived to take them to Christine's office, she led them down a grand staircase with silver handrails, just like the ones he'd seen in the movie *Titanic*.

He was relieved when they were shown into an office that, although it had a stunning view of the whole waterfront, was of modest proportions.

"Hi, Liz," said Christine, jumping up from behind the desk. "Hello, Mr. Quan." Henry was taken aback for an instant by her height. An attractive woman, she was wearing a smart turquoise business suit that perfectly set off her shining dark eyes.

"Look," she said, "I'm just back from vacation and I've got a thousand things on the go. Just give me a minute and I'll be with you."

Liz and Henry admired the view, studiously avoiding listening in on Christine as she made a couple of calls.

"Down there," Henry told Liz, pointing. "That's where I got mixed up in that student demonstration."

> **THE SCREW TIGHTENS**
>
> *"By the mid-1990s, student fees were less affordable for an average family than at any time during the previous twenty years."*
>
> Source: *StatsCan*

"You did!" said Christine over her shoulder. "Honest to God, I could hear the noise from right up here. It sounded pretty frightening."

In a few minutes, she was ready.

"Beautiful kids," said Liz, indicating the picture of two toddlers on Christine's desk. "What are their names?"

"Trevor and Michael. Aren't they sweeties?"

"Are you saving for their university years?" Henry inquired as Christine marched ahead of them towards the elevators.

"You bet," she replied over her shoulder. "I saw a lot of my friends in the early nineties spending all this money on doodads for their kids. I mean, who needs ten Barbies? And it occurred to me, this spending is all for the adults. All this stuff they're buying, it's going to end up in the landfill. But how on earth are they going to pay for their kids' education?"

"It's true," said Liz as they got on the elevator. "We spoil them when they're young, but it's later we should be thinking about."

With Christine pressed for time, they settled on a salad-and-sandwich bar in the shopping mall beneath the tower.

"I just had three kids join our department right out of school," said the unstoppable Christine as they carried their lunches to a table. "I was asking them, and one of them has a $20,000 student loan to pay off, another $25,000, and the third is just getting married and, between them, she and her husband, who is a law clerk, owe $30,000. And I'm asking myself, where are these kids going to find the money to buy homes, have kids, spring for the $40,000 Jeep everyone says they should have? Economically, it doesn't make sense. It blew my mind. These kids — and their parents — grew up thinking everything was going to be free, like Sweden. And don't get the idea that just because they're working for a mutual-fund company, they're making millions. They're in graphic arts, PR, and they're getting around $28,000."

"But, Christine," said Liz, jumping in as her friend stopped to fork in a mouthful of salad, "don't a lot of people have savings plans? What about RESPs? . . . Is that what they're called?"

"Registered education savings plans?" The others were afraid for a moment she'd choke. "They've been a real bust. Check the figures — less than 3 percent of kids going through university are making use of RESPs. Okay, so now the finance minister has made some big changes. If your kid doesn't go to university, for instance, you may be able to transfer the money into your RRSP. We'll have to see if RESPs are a better deal in future."

"Don't parents *want* to save for their children's education?" asked Henry.

"They say they do," replied Christine. "But if you ask them what they're doing, they say, 'Nothing.' Because later on they expect to be able to pay for it."

"Well, hasn't that always worked in the past?" asked Liz.

"If you believe that, why are all these kids landing on the street with big debts around their necks? And it's going to get worse. For heaven's sake, look at how the cost of a university education is going up. Tuition is up 152 percent in the last ten years. You've seen the figures. Just on the basis of 3 percent inflation, my husband and I will be looking at total costs of $67,000 for each of our kids when they're ready to enrol. 'And what happens,' I ask these parents, 'if they lose their jobs at forty-five?' It happened to a lot of people in our generation, Liz."

"And grandparents?" said Henry. "What should they be doing?"

"Now that's interesting, Mr. Quan." Christine, who had finished her salad, turned to face him. "Grandparents are always buying their grandchildren goodies, right?"

Henry smiled, blushing a little.

"Every month there's a holiday or a birthday. If you've got kids, you open the door and there are more presents all the time.

"Now if the grandparents said, 'Look, we won't buy any more presents.'" She caught the look of alarm in Henry's eye. "Well, just a few! But if, instead of buying presents, they put $500 a year in a savings fund, in seventeen years that becomes $17,000."

"But that's a long way from the $67,000 you say they'll need."

"Gotcha. But it's a start. It will pay for the first year at school. If you really want to know, though, I can give you the perfect answer for grandparents. If they put $5,000 in a fund when the child is born, that's $50,000 by the time the kid needs it to go to school. Put $10,000 in, and you never have to think about it again. There'll be enough money and more besides."

"How can that be?" asked Henry sceptically. "That's not a whole lot of money."

"The magic ingredient — time!" said Christine with a note of triumph. "I couldn't believe it myself, so I asked someone to check the figures for me. Know what $10,000 would be worth today if you'd put it in one of our funds in 1981?"

"What?" they said together.

"A hundred and fifty-two thousand dollars, that's what! That's your $67,000, plus you could buy two cars with what's left over. All right, all right!" she laughed as Liz went to challenge her. "I know. That's hindsight. No one can tell what the stock market will do in the future. But my point is, the market has delivered good returns historically, and given a time-scale of fifteen or twenty years, that $10,000 investment — or regular payments over a period of time — should mean the money's there when the kid needs it.

"Basically, you have three choices," said Christine as they walked out of the restaurant. "If you want to put your kid through school, you can do pay-as-you-go. Even for a couple with a $75,000 income — $58,000 after taxes — that's a big hit. It means they must come up with $7,000 to $10,000 a year for four years. Ouch!

"You could choose to pay the shot after by taking out a loan. But with interest, that could even double your total cost. Or, and I don't have to tell you which one I like, you can pay ahead of time and it will cost you only a fraction of the money."

"And what does your research tell you most people will do?" asked Liz.

"Most people?" said Christine, pressing the button for the elevator. "They won't do a damned thing. They'll sit on their duffs and expect their kids to pay. And at the end, the kids face an impossible choice: to start their lives with a burden of debt or — and this is what worries me — not to go to school at all."

"It sounds simple enough, Chris," said Liz, "but how many grandparents can afford to plonk down that much money? Most of them are worried about not having enough for retirement."

"You'd be surprised how many could afford it," said Christine. "Don't forget, as the Baby Boomers' parents pass on, we're seeing the biggest transfer of assets ever. It's in the billions. And wouldn't it make sense for some of these older folks to put a little money into the younger generation instead of hanging on to it until the bitter end?"

"I guess so," mumbled Henry. "So why don't they?"

"I tell you, sometimes I could scream. The reason nearly always is that we're so tight-assed — pardon my French, Mr. Quan — about talking about money. Sex and money are the two big taboos in the Canadian family. We don't discuss our finances with our parents and, heaven forbid, our parents don't talk about the money they've got. So, damn it, it's okay to buy the kid a piece of space junk, but we never get around to talking about what will really matter in their lives."

◆

Are Canadian parents slouches when it comes to saving for their children's post-secondary education? The evidence is not encouraging. Parents show a high degree of concern, but not much follow-through.

When the Angus Reid Group polled more than a thousand parents in the fall of 1996, it found that while 77 percent of parents with children under eight intend to start a savings plan, only 24 percent of parents with kids at university actually did so.

It's not for lack of concern. The poll showed that a substantial 82 percent were concerned about having money to pay for their children's education. But when it came right down to it, contributing to an RESP came a poor third on their priority list (with a score of 19 percent),

NO CHOICE FOR BETTER-OFF PARENTS

When your kid applies for a student loan, you could find yourself on the hook. In the needs test, parental incomes are examined. A family with two children and an income of less than $50,000 would not be expected to contribute. But where family income is $80,000, Mom and Dad are expected to kick in $8,000. If both children are taking post-secondary studies, the $8,000 would be divided between them. But by saving ahead of time, you can avoid or lessen that sting.

behind paying off the mortgage (50 percent) and contributing to an RRSP (27 percent). The poll, conducted for Trimark Mutual Funds, also showed that parents' earlier expectations rarely measured up when the time came for their kids to go to university. While 13 percent of parents with kids eight years and under thought an RESP would help pay their offspring's way through school, only 2 percent of those with children actually attending university reported using an RESP.

Again, 22 percent of parents with younger children anticipated they would be able to help pay for school out of their savings, but the reality was that only 10 percent were able to do so when the time came.

The parents with younger children only got the question right when more than a third of them said they thought they would have to pay university costs out of their after-tax income. In fact, 37 percent of parents with youngsters at university were footing bills out of their take-home pay — a crippling blow to the family budget — while 48 percent of those whose children had graduated reported they'd had to dip into their day-to-day income to find the money.

So where did the rest of the money come from? The figures tell a disheartening story. Only 9 percent of parents of younger kids thought they would have to rely on student loans. In fact, today about 60 percent of students must rely on loans.

Few parents, too, had anticipated that their kids would have to work their way through school; in the event, a quarter of those attending university were paying out of their own earnings.

Again, under the heading Talking Big, when the parents were asked if they were likely to save for or contribute to a grandchild's education, 65 percent answered aye. As most would not have grandchildren yet, there's no way of knowing if they will really follow through. But with most older Canadians worried about saving for their retirement, it seems likely the kids will get short shrift from Grandma and Grandpa.

Canadian parents, too, it turned out, are sadly unsophisticated when it comes to saving effectively for their children's education. By far the biggest proportion (34 percent) of those who had saved or intended to save mentioned savings accounts as their first choice. In this low-interest era, that's about as effective in growth and tax-efficiency terms as putting your money in a sock! While RESPs were second (15 percent), Canada Savings Bonds, only marginally better than a straight savings account, scored third, with 13 percent.

No wonder we're facing a crisis!

Chapter 5

Scholarships: Give Your Kid an Edge

*H*enry was intrigued. For the last hour, sitting on the dock with his line dangling in the water, he had been aware of the man in hip waders trolling back and forth in the lake. Occasionally, the fellow would stop and reach down into the murky, knee-deep water, evidently looking for something.

"What are you after?" Henry asked finally.

"Eh?" The man took off his earphones.

"What are you looking for?"

"Oh, money, jewellery. You'd be surprised what ends up on the bottom of the lake during the tourist season."

"What is that instrument you're holding?"

"A metal detector. I can tell by the sound in my earphones if there's something there."

"Do you ever find anything of value?" Before the man could answer, Henry felt the splatter of the first fat raindrops falling from a sky that had been growing steadily darker for the last ten minutes.

"We're gonna have to give up," the man said. "Care to shelter in Skipper's? It might clear up. Looks as if you've had no better luck than me," he commented as Henry gathered up his tackle box and his empty bucket.

By the time they had crossed the road to the coffee bar,

the rain had developed into a downpour. As he always did when he went fishing at Lake Simcoe, Henry had brought along his raincoat, but it was in the car, and now his sweater felt damp.

"Hot cup of coffee? We need it!"

Henry nodded. "Thanks."

"You were asking if I ever found anything valuable," the man said as he sat down with the coffees. "Found an old cannon once. And just a few weeks ago, a silver bracelet. I wouldn't say it was priceless, though."

"Do you make your living at it?"

The man, fortyish with dark hair, gave a booming laugh. "No way. It's just a hobby. But it's not so different from my everyday job."

"What is that?" Henry asked.

"I hunt for treasure," he replied.

Henry looked puzzled. "You mean you go diving on shipwrecks, something like that?"

"No, nothing so dangerous. I am a high-school teacher. Mike Howell is my name," he said, holding out his hand.

"Henry Quan. But where is the treasure?" he inquired.

"Everywhere you can imagine. It's all around us. There for the finding," Howell said mysteriously. Then he explained.

◆

Our research for this book would not have been complete without a visit to the district high school in Sutton, Ontario, where Mike Howell is not only a teacher, but also a scholarship coach. Howell's influence, though, is felt across the country in a series of books, one for each region, called *Winning Scholarships: A Student's Guide to Entrance Awards at Universities and Colleges* (University of Toronto Press).

Howell believes, and we concur, that with university costs rising dramatically, the best-prepared students will have a *portfolio* of financial resources to fall back on. Our book explains how parents and grandparents can achieve dramatic results by saving early and selecting the most efficient investment vehicles. For those students whose families don't save, or don't save enough, the alternatives by the time they reach university age are usually to borrow or take a job (or both), choices that may take away from the quality of a post-secondary education and leave the graduating student weighed down under a burden of debt.

Howell argues, though, that most students and their high schools are ignoring an important third source of funds. There is a huge pot of scholarship money out there to be won, he says.

"I have found millions of dollars sitting in plain view," he writes in the introduction to the latest edition of one of his books. Amazingly, a lot of scholarship money sits uncollected year after year because students and teachers are not aware of it. In hunting for scholarship treasure, says Howell, students stand not only to improve their financial situation at university, but also to give themselves the inside track on getting into the schools and courses they want.

WHERE PEOPLE VOLUNTEER

People most often volunteer among the following groups:

religious organizations
  – 17 percent
sports and recreation
  – 16 percent
education and youth
  – 14 percent
health
  – 10 percent
social service
  – 9 percent
community service
  – 8 percent

In February 1998, Finance Minister Paul Martin announced the granddaddy of all scholarships: the $2.5 billion Millennium Scholarship Fund. Starting in the year 2000, the fund will hand out one hundred thousand scholarships a year worth about $3,000 each. Martin envisaged that the fund would run out in about ten years — a short-sighted idea, in our view, that will penalize children of Romney Anderson-Quan's generation, who will not be eligible. However, we would not be surprised to see the Millennium Fund still distributing its largesse twenty years from now, which means that Howell's advice on winning scholarships will continue to be indispensable.

A note on terminology: bursaries and scholarships are sometimes confused. Bursaries are usually given to needy students past the first year of university. Scholarships are generally awarded on merit and are granted regardless of the parents' income, although lately some scholarships also consider financial need. The Millennium Fund appears to be one of these hybrids.

Who gives scholarships? Everyone you could imagine. Most are funnelled through universities, although all sorts of companies and organizations offer them. They can range from a $500 award from the Girl Guides of Canada to the $26,000 (over four years) Trent University President's Scholarship. Nationally, says Howell, British Columbia offers the most scholarships, with Alberta second. Manitoba is at the bottom of the list.

Scholarships all too often have amounted to charity for the well-to-do. Because it is the children of middle-class, university-educated parents who are most likely to go to university, these kids were also most likely to win scholarships. The wealthy and the powerful have always sought to give their kids an edge — as well as access to the best schools and the best scholarships — by sending them to private schools. In the United Kingdom, for instance, for generations the two senior universities, Oxford and Cambridge, were almost the exclusive preserve of what we would call private-school graduates (although that is not as true today). In more egalitarian Canada, that has generally not been the case, although there are still plenty of parents who believe private school — or independent schools, as they are called these days — confer an advantage. In 1996, there were 276,185 students enrolled in independent schools, 5.5 percent of Canada's student population, although that total also includes many religious schools.

Do they offer a better education? There are no hard and fast figures (although some private schools, including Ontario's prestigious Upper Canada College, are now beginning to offer the International Baccalaureate, an internationally recognized standard of excellence, which will provide a clearer basis for comparison in the future).

Gary Duthler, executive director of the Federation of Independent Schools in Canada, says some private schools perform poorly, and it's up to parents to visit the school, talk to other parents with children at the school, and discover for themselves whether the school is suitable for their child.

"There is no way you will ever know you have got the best school," he admits. What independent schools offer, he says, is choice, especially in areas like Calgary, where a rigid school system offers only a one-track brand of schooling.

Back in Sutton, Mike Howell believes the real advantage the best private schools offer is a single-minded dedication to winning scholarships. "It's their secret," he told us. "They have to do it to justify the $8,000 to $14,000 parents are paying." And the beautiful thing is, says Howell, that you, as a parent, can play a part in having your own community school adopt the successful methods used by the schools where bank presidents and tycoons tend to send their kids.

We thought, perhaps like you, that scholarships were handed out strictly to the kids with the highest marks, so if you were not the smartest kid in the school you did not stand a chance. How could we have been so naïve?

Howell (who, in his spare time, does indeed troll for treasure in Lake Simcoe with his metal detector) explained that scholarships are awarded for a thousand different reasons, and the trick is to match the kid to the scholarship. And surprise, surprise, universities, he says, are as interested in recruiting well-rounded individuals who will play a part in the school community as they are in admitting scholars.

Sutton and District High School, where these two principles are part of the school dogma, is not the sort of place where you find Jaguars and BMWs in the parking-lot. The school, the biggest building in town, serves a depressed, mainly rural area eighty kilometres north of Toronto that relies on the tourist trade and where many families are on social assistance. But the guidance department, where Howell and Dr. Judith Ryan, the head of guidance, work their magic, simply hums.

There's a big board on the wall with all the scholarship-application deadlines marked, and Dr. Ryan opened a filing cabinet for us in which she has details on hundreds of scholarships, many in the names of Canadians both famous and unknown. All are colour-coded: red for those available to students with disabilities, pink for Native scholarships, blue for those offered by the Canadian Union of Public Employees, and so on.

"Are you East Indian, Catholic?" she said. "The fact is there's hardly a student who doesn't qualify for a special scholarship. The money is there."

Adds Howell, "It's not about marks; it's about the whole person."

True enough. Just examine the eligibility criteria for one of the plums of the scholarship scene: twenty Canada Trust Community Leadership scholarships worth $14,000 plus the full cost of tuition over four years. They are open, says the company, "to students who have demonstrated outstanding community leadership, either in their school community, the community at large, or both." Academic qualifications are mentioned second.

Ryan explains, "We tell them, you can get a mark of ninety-eight, but if you're not involved, it won't count [in winning a scholarship]."

So how does Sutton, a school of 1,650 in an area where most parents did not go to college, let alone university, motivate its kids? When youngsters arrive in Grade Nine, Ryan and Howell meet with them in small groups to impart some shocking news: marks do not count — not until the later grades, anyway. In their first year or two in high school, because they are younger and smaller, students tend to hang back, "hiding their heads in their lockers until they're bigger," said Howell. "We tell them to get their heads out of the locker and get involved from the start." These are the years of exploration, they're told, and they are handed a high-school planner on which they can record their extracurricular activities and achievements. They're encouraged to become active in school clubs, committees, and activities like the school band, the theatre group, anything that really interests them. They are also reminded that every community has its share of volunteer organizations, from Greenpeace to their neighbourhood church to the Rotary Club, and that volunteer work will count big when it comes to scholarship applications. The Canadian Armed Forces Reserves also offer, not only a host of activities for teenagers, but also paid summer employment that will help them through college or university later on.

The Duke of Edinburgh Awards, the ultimate program for encouraging student initiative, is also ideal for youngsters with their hearts on scholarships, and if your school does not have a DEA group, Howell suggests you speak to a favourite teacher about it. A favourite teacher, indeed, is part of the overall game plan. Howell urges kids to latch on to a teacher they admire and treat him or her as their mentor — someone they can take their problems to and with whom they can discuss their plans and dreams.

The school, too, comes out a winner: the heavy concentration on extracurricular activities in the earlier years means there is a constantly renewed pool of student leadership talent.

No time for all those activities? Howell issues students with a pizza-shaped diagram with every slice representing one of the twenty-four hours of the day. Somewhere in there, he tells them, is a "golden hour" that could be put to better use.

Students, though, are discouraged from dipping into an activity for a few weeks just so they can put it on their sheet. Selection committees soon see through that ploy, and are more interested in boys and girls who have progressed through an organization, perhaps to an executive position.

Special mention must be made of students with disabilities and for whom the scholarship field is a particularly fruitful one. The National Educational Association of Disabled Students (NEADS) in Ottawa publishes an extensive list of scholarships on its Web site, www.indie.ca/neads/, and its executive director, Frank Smith, says he is also hopeful that there will be provision in the Millennium Fund for disabled students, who are often the neediest.

Sutton parents are also brought in on the game plan for success and are reminded that, although work experience is useful, if their son or daughter is busy every night slinging hamburgers, it means there's little time for the activities that could spell success later. Many of the parents become highly motivated in the chase for scholarship money, wanting to see their kids get a better chance than they did.

Mention scholarships and a lot of parents and students, influenced by the American example, think of football or hockey scholarships. They are not a significant factor in Canada, however. Sports activities are great, Howell believes, but a too-heavy involvement in hockey during high school can be a drawback for the youngster seeking a university future. "I think it roughens kids and makes them anti-school," he said. "Also, it takes them away from school a lot on playing trips."

Figure skating, that other pet Canadian parental preoccupation, also tends to take up too much of a youngster's time, leaving little room for the variety of activities that produces a rounded person with the social skills to succeed. It must be mentioned, though, that the Canadian Figure Skating Association offers $8,000 Athlete Trust Scholarships to young skaters who win gold medals in Canadian championship qualifying events.

Competitive golf can also provide a path to that place in university. There are twenty Canadian Golf Foundation Scholarship Awards for young players with competitive experience, each worth up to $20,000.

> **IN LINE FOR MILLENNIUM MONEY**
> *Who will be eligible for Canada's $2.5 billion Millennium Fund? The same 550,000 students (out of a total of 1.3 million) who now qualify for student loans. It is unlikely the scholarships will be available for families whose incomes exceed $55,000 a year.*

Grades Nine and Ten, say Ryan and Howell, are the years of exploration and discovery, when getting off to a good start in high school is more important than getting top marks. The kid who gets ninety in Grade Nine may, said Howell, be a burn-out by Grade Twelve, figuring that she hasn't had any fun in school and that it's time to break out. By the final year, with a solid core of activities behind them, students can concentrate on the marks they will need to qualify on academic terms.

At this point scholarship-hunting goes into high gear. Ryan calls students down to her office to let them know of awards they might be in the running for, application forms are handed out and then, because each school is generally allowed only one nominee for a particular scholarship, a staff committee will pick the candidate it thinks has the best chance. Candidates are kept abreast of scholarship deadlines and go through mock interviews with staff members so they'll feel more confident when they go for their scholarship interview. Many report the eventual interview is less gruelling than the mock affair at school.

Does the system work? "We're getting regular winners," reported Howell. "Kids good enough to go up against the best in the country — and win." A school like Sutton may even hold an advantage for a smart, motivated kid. In the best private schools and in city schools in high-income areas, there are lots of children who are receiving a heap of encouragement from home, so there may be intense competition to be nominated for the one shot the school has at a scholarship. In a regular high school, there is more opportunity for the kid with ambitions. It's the big-fish-in-a-little-pond principle.

Howell pointed to two recent examples of Sutton students for whom scholarships have paid off in multiple ways. Jennifer Couturier, a student with a bent for science, decided to apply for every scholarship she was qualified for, and was offered a total of more than $50,000 by several universities. She picked Queen's, in Kingston, Ontario, collecting $20,000 over four years and covering about half of her total university costs. With that money behind her, and using the approach she had learned so well at Sutton, she worked as a volunteer at a Kingston hospital. It is unusual for a B.Sc. graduate to be offered a place in medical school right off, but with her volunteering background and good marks, Jennifer was offered places at two prestigious medical schools when she applied. Carl Rothfels graduated from Sutton in 1996 after winning two Junior Citizen of the Year awards and went to McMaster University with $30,000 in scholarships. In his case, said Howell, it meant he had to borrow money only when it came time for his master's degree. With his background, said Howell, he also stands a good chance of getting a job as a teaching assistant — another means of paying your way painlessly through university.

"Even if I hadn't won any scholarships," Rothfels writes, "I would still be glad to have gone through the process. I learned a great deal about time management, meeting deadlines, expressing myself, and improving my presentation skills."

And missing out on a scholarship may not be all bad news,

said Howell. Scholarship committees often pass on the word, so a student who did not win will still have the inside track when it comes to securing a place in that university in the course desired.

So why are universities so intent on getting "rounded" students rather than bookworms? "Universities are like little towns," said Howell. "They are looking for real community members who will get involved in their activities, not robots." The pay-off for the university, he said, is that these are the very students most likely to succeed in life, and the ones who can be expected to donate later to alumni funds. They may, in turn, even set up scholarship funds themselves. And there's another reason universities look beyond marks. In recent years, certain high schools have become notorious for inflating marks, but an activity record is harder to fake.

SCHOLARSHIPS GROW

Universities, according to Statistics Canada, boosted spending on awards by 4.3 percent in 1996, and it's estimated that the number of students receiving scholarships has climbed from one in ten a decade ago to one in eight today. The University of Alberta tripled its recruitment scholarship fund in three years to $1.9 million, while Simon Fraser University, in British Columbia, upped theirs from $700,000 to $3.2 million over the past five years.

Some schools, especially the private ones, like to keep quiet about their scholarship programs, not wanting to encourage too much competition for the coveted prizes. Not Sutton. Its principal and staff believe in sounding the trumpet for scholarships every way they know how. There are point systems and trophies for school activities ("A school without trophies is a dead school," says Howell), scholarship certificates won by outstanding grads hang outside the principal's office, and the local newspaper is kept informed of any scholarship successes.

Ryan and Howell also respond to the many calls they receive from other high schools asking for information about their program, and they have given workshops on the methods they use. Whenever he's invited to speak at a high school, Howell asks his audience: "Do you have a basketball coach?" The answer is usually a big yes. "Do you have a football coach?" Next question: "Is that because the kids will go on to play football or basketball professionally?" Silence. Final question: "And do you have a scholarship coach?" Point made.

What can parents do to groom their kids for success? Although winning scholarships takes a lot of motivation, the first thing Howell tells parents is not to try to impose perfection. "Don't push them beyond the enjoyment level," he says, "or they will end up feeling bad about themselves."

Some of Howell's pointers for parents:
- Make sure your child has a quiet, well-lit, well-ventilated room in which to study.
- Let them choose the study hour, but have them stick to it without telephone and other interruptions.
- Don't be afraid to check on their work habits or to talk to their teachers.
- In addition to praise for your child's achievement, don't hesitate to call and thank a teacher for special help or an outstanding teaching effort.
- Limit part-time student jobs to weekends and to no more than fifteen hours a week.
- It's expensive, but the reality is every student really needs a computer these days. You are only preparing them for the computer world ahead of them.

If your children's high school does not have a scholarship program, Howell says you should press for one through the parents' association. And check every organization you are connected with to see if they offer scholarships for members' children. Trade unions, credit unions, the Legion, service clubs — all are just dying to give money to deserving students. Other sources of scholarship info? Canadian Guidance Services, of Burlington, Ontario, offers a guide: *Scholarship*, by Brian Harris, on its Web site www.worldchat.com/commercial/canguide/index.html. University and college Web sites are also valuable resources.

◆

The clouds had receded, the sun was out again, and steam rose from the dock as Henry rigged up his stool and rebaited his hook.

"I will remember everything you have said," he told Howell, who was checking out his metal detector.

"How old is your granddaughter?"

"She's not one yet."

"Never too early to start."

Henry laughed. "I don't think she's ready to apply for a scholarship yet."

"But you would be surprised how early they learn to compete. And you can start them early. It can be as easy as a contest for children in the newspaper or filling out ballots at the supermarket. I hear kids talking about luck. Well, there is fortuitous luck and there's the luck you make yourself. Someone has to win — it might as well be you."

Henry tensed. "A bite! I've got a bite," he said.

"See what I mean," said his companion. "Here's the net."

Chapter 6

What's Theirs Is Yours — Sometimes

*T*he idea seemed so simple.

"We just put a little money aside each month," Henry explained to Mary after dinner one evening. It was their time for serious talk, after the dishes had been picked up and the leftovers stored away in the fridge.

"Look, I have it all figured out." He produced a sheet of paper covered with numbers. "If we can afford just $50 a month, we can save $600 a year for little Romney. Then, every year, we use the money to buy her a Canada Savings Bond. They're paying about 4 percent this year. By the time she's ready for college, there should be plenty of money."

Mary nodded, but he could see the concern in her face.

"What? What is it? You don't like the idea?"

"It's just that $50 doesn't seem like much when you say it. But where do we find that money? We barely have enough now."

"We will find it. It's important. Young children today must have a good education if they are to succeed. There are lots of ways we can save. Maybe we'll stop taking the cable. We hardly ever watch the television anyway."

"But I thought you said there would be some money for Romney when we sell the store," Mary said.

"We should never count on these things until we have the money in our hands," Henry replied. "I've heard that a lot of these big real-estate deals come to nothing. The company goes bankrupt or something. So we can't depend on it. Or it may be years before it happens. We need to start saving now."

Mary looked dubious, but said nothing. When Henry got an idea, it was hard to change his mind, especially where the children, and now a grandchild, were concerned.

Two days later, Henry announced that maybe his idea wasn't such a good one after all.

"Why not?" she asked.

Henry shook his head. "Canada is a strange country. Do you know that even if you want to give something away, the government may not let you? Not even to your own child or grandchild!"

"How can that be?" Mary exclaimed. "This is supposed to be a free land. How can the government stop you from making a gift to your grandchild?"

"Actually, they don't really stop you," Henry said. "They just make you pay taxes on the money even after you've given it away. I read all about it today in the newspaper."

◆

What Henry had seen was a story that outlined the country's strange and often convoluted income-attribution rules. These are regulations developed by the Federal Department of Finance and administered by Revenue Canada that are intended to prevent wealthy people from avoiding taxes by simply transferring assets to other family members. Unfortunately, middle- and lower-income people also get caught up in the same net.

Here's how it works. Let's say you give a sum of money to your child and he or she invests it in mutual funds. For tax purposes, the government has decreed that any interest or dividends generated by those mutual funds is attributed back to you for tax purposes. So if Henry invested $600 in a Canada Savings Bond for Romney and it earned 4 percent in a year, the $24 of interest it generated would have to be added on to his taxable income when he prepared his return. That

YOU WILL PAY

If you give money to a child or grandchild to invest, any interest or dividend earned is attributed to you for tax purposes. This rule also extends to other close relatives, such as nephews and nieces.

may not seem like a lot, but if they kept up the savings plan, over time it would add several hundred dollars a year to their tax bill.

These income-attribution rules apply to several family members, including spouses, but Henry was most concerned by their application to minor children. The article, quoting from an official Revenue Canada Interpretation Bulletin (No. IT-510), said that the rules apply to any child "or other descendant" under age eighteen. That means it extends to grandchildren, great-grandchildren, and on down. Nieces and nephews are also covered under the same prohibitions.

The rules are broadly worded to cover loans, gifts, and any other transfers of money or assets.

However, and Henry was especially interested in this, the author of the article, a chartered accountant, pointed out some interesting ways around the rules. For one, he noted that paragraph four of the bulletin specifically states that any income earned on reinvested interest or dividends will be considered to belong to the child for tax purposes. The attribution rules cut off at that stage.

Going back to the $600 in Canada Savings Bonds, that meant the first $24 in interest would be Henry and Mary's for tax purposes until Romney turned eighteen. But if that $24 was reinvested, future interest on it, and the interest earned on *that* interest, would not be taxed in their hands. The money would be considered to be Romney's for tax purposes, but since she wasn't likely to be earning any other income, it wouldn't matter. If CSBs continued to pay 4 percent, the original $24 would grow to almost $45 over the next sixteen years. Of course, if they repeated the process every year, the amount would be much more substantial.

A second loophole touched on in the article concerned relatives living outside Canada, who do not come under the jurisdiction of our tax laws. If an aunt or uncle or some other relation living in another country decided to give money to a child in Canada to set up an education fund, no income-attribution rules would apply. Of course, the author noted, the gift must be a genuine one, not a sham created for purposes of tax evasion.

> **FOREIGN RESIDENTS ARE EXEMPT**
> *Money given by relatives living outside Canada is not subject to the attribution rules because the givers don't pay taxes in this country.*

Reading that section of the story, Henry had thought for a moment about his sister in Hong Kong. But no, they actually had to send her a little bit of money from time to time to help out. She had no resources to assist Romney. As for Mary's aunt and uncle in Canton, they were even worse off, despite improving economic conditions in China. No solution there.

But the final point in the article looked more promising. The accountant noted that while the attribution rules apply to dividends and interest, capital gains and losses are specifically excluded. That creates a huge loophole, he pointed out. A parent or grandparent could give money to a child and direct that it be invested in a security that would likely produce only capital gains, such as a stock or equity mutual fund. That way, all the profits stay in the hands of the child and are not attributed back to the original giver.

◆

"But capital gains, Henry? Doesn't that mean the stock market? Isn't there a lot of risk involved in that? What's the point of us sacrificing to save money if there's a chance it will all be lost anyway?" Mary asked.

> **CAPITAL GAINS BELONG TO THE CHILD**
> *Unlike interest and dividend income, capital gains are considered to belong to the child for tax purposes. This loophole provides an option for parents to invest for a child's education outside an RESP.*

Henry had to agree. He, too, was conservative by nature. The only thing worse than giving his money to the government in taxes would be to see it all lost in one of those terrible stock-market crashes he had heard about. Of course, he had never invested in stocks — there had never been any extra money for that sort of thing — but he had heard the stories.

He sighed. He would have to look for another way. There was no problem that did not have a solution — even if the solution wasn't always apparent.

Chapter 7

Saving the Child Tax Benefit

"*I* just found it today," said Liz, shifting Romney to her other arm. "It must have got mixed up with my other papers when I came home from the hospital." She handed the official-looking form across the table to Jeff. "It sounds as if we have some money coming to us."

"The Child Tax Benefit," Jeff read. "You're right. There could be something here. What do you think, Dad?"

It was a happy occasion, the first time Liz had felt up to cooking the family Sunday dinner since Romney's birth. Henry had bought a bottle of sparkling wine to celebrate and they had drunk a toast to long life, happiness, and success for the youngster.

The time after dinner, as it had always been in the Quan household, was devoted to discussing family business matters.

"It was only when I saw it that I remembered," said Liz, as Jeff handed the form to his father. "They told me at the hospital to fill it out and send it away to Ottawa right away. I guess with so much on my mind . . . I hope we don't miss out on some cheques."

"Hmm," Henry said, noncommittally. He was by nature suspicious of anything emanating from government, at whatever level. "There's probably a catch somewhere. There always is."

◆

HEALTHY BENEFITS
*The Child Tax
Benefit provides
basic payments of
$1,020 annually
for the first child,
with the amount
increasing with the
number of children.*

He was right — and wrong. The Child Tax Benefit (CTB) is designed to provide financial support to lower-income families. It is the successor to the old Family Allowance program, the so-called Baby Bonus, which gave government cheques to everyone with children.

The CTB is more targeted, directing the money to those who need it most. The payments are gradually phased out as income rises. As a result, families with higher income may receive little or nothing under the plan.

The basic Child Tax Benefit works as follows. Any family with a net income of less than $25,921 will receive a full payment, based on this scale:

One child	$1,020 a year
Two children	$2,040 a year
Three children	$3,135 a year
Four children	$4,230 a year

Besides that, children under age seven are eligible for an additional $213 if no child care tax credit is claimed for them.

Once income passes the threshold, the amount of the payment is reduced by 2.5 percent of additional income for one-child families and 5 percent for larger families. So if your family income is $1,000 over the threshold and you have one child, your payment will be reduced by $25 (2.5% x $1,000 = $25). If you have two or more children, you lose $50 (5% x $1,000 = $50).

As well, an additional supplement was introduced in July 1998 for very low income families. They receive an extra $605 for the first child, $405 for the second, and $330 for the third child and beyond. Families with incomes below $20,921 will receive the full amount. Beyond that, the payment will be reduced by 12.1 percent of any excess income for one-child families, 20.2 percent for those with two children, and 26.8 percent for families with three or more youngsters. For example, if you have one child and your family income exceeds $20,921 by $1,000, you will lose $121 of the supplement (12.1% x $1,000 = $121). If you have two children, you'll lose $202 (20.2% x $1,000 = $202).

When net family income reaches $25,921, no supplement will be paid; however, the regular Child Tax Benefit will still apply, with reductions as income rises beyond that level.

In the case of Jeff and Liz, they would be eligible for the full amount including the supplement. Jeff was earning just under $20,000 a year in his entry-level computer job, while Liz had taken a prolonged leave of absence from the law firm where she worked to have Romney and decide whether she wanted to mix family and career.

Liz had been given a copy of Revenue Canada form RC66, entitled the Child Tax Benefit Application. With it came a pamphlet explaining the program.

◆

> **PAYMENT PHASE-OUT**
> *Supplemental Child Tax Benefit payments start to be phased out when family net income surpasses $20,921 a year. The more children you have, the faster the payment is clawed back.*

"We should be eligible for the full amount, at least for the time being," Jeff said. "That would really help us out, with Liz not working."

"Hmm." Henry continued to read through the information. Something was nagging at the back of his mind, something he had read or heard about this program. He kept casting about in his brain, but it just wouldn't come to him.

◆

What it was, as he eventually recalled, was a unique tax rule relating to money from the Child Tax Benefit, a hold-over from the Family Allowance days. If the money is invested in trust on behalf of the child, any income earned is considered to be the youngster's for tax purposes. The income-attribution rules do not apply.

When the Child Tax Benefit was first brought in, the government announced that rule would be changed. But after reconsideration, that decision was scrapped and the Child

Tax Credit was given the same status for investment purposes as the Family Allowance.

So Jeff and Liz could invest the $1,625 a year they would receive for Romney in an education fund and not have to worry about the tax implications. It seemed like the perfect solution.

NO INCOME ATTRIBUTION

If Child Tax Benefit payments are invested on a youngster's behalf, any interest and dividends earned are considered to belong to the child for tax purposes. Normal income-attribution rules do not apply.

◆

Over the next week, Henry did a variety of calculations. When Jeff, Liz, and Romney came to see him and Mary the following Sunday, Henry was ready with his numbers as soon as the table was cleared.

"Look at this," he said excitedly. "You can open up an account for Romney at the bank and invest the full amount every year. You don't even have to pay tax on the money when you get it." He shook his head wonderingly; it was so unlike the Canadian government not to tax every cent.

He ran his finger down the columns of numbers. "You can put the money into a GIC for her. They're paying about 5 percent a year. See what happens?"

Jeff ran his eye down the page. Henry had calculated that Romney would have more than $20,000 after ten years. By the time she turned eighteen, the cut-off age for the program, the total would be in excess of $45,000.

Henry beamed. "See! More than enough to send her to college." He looked so pleased with himself that Jeff hesitated to say anything. Still, they had always been forthright with one another.

"That's great, Dad. Thanks for doing this. It's just that . . ."

"What? What?"

"Well, for one thing, we're pretty tight for cash right now, with Liz not working and all. That extra money would really help us out. It costs a lot of money to have a baby, as we're learning awfully fast. I really don't think we could afford to put all that government money into an account for her."

"But you'll be earning more money soon. That company

you're with, they're going places. What is it they do? Internet sales?"

"Sure they are, but Dad, as my income goes up, the government money will go down, and fast. If Liz goes back to work, and we've been talking about that, it'll drop to zero in no time."

"So you're telling us that you have to stay poor to get this money, in which case you can't afford to save it?" Mary injected herself into the discussion for the first time; she'd left it to Henry until now, but she could see he was becoming upset with Jeff's rejection of the idea.

"Just about." Jeff looked at her with relief. He didn't want to hurt his father. "Look at it this way, Dad," he said, turning back to Henry. "The government has done its usual trick of giving with one hand and taking away with the other."

Henry brightened at that. It was just as he had always said, never trust a politician. "So I guess we'll have to find another way," he said.

"I guess so," Jeff agreed. "Nice try though, Dad."

> **CAN YOU AFFORD TO SAVE?**
> *The problem with basing an education-savings program on the Child Tax Benefit is that most low-income families will have more urgent needs for the money. And if their income rises in the future, the payments will be diminished or vanish entirely.*

Chapter 8

Looking for Loopholes

*H*enry's mistrust of governments went back a long way. He had seen too many examples of abuse and corruption in his lifetime to feel comfortable with the actions of political leaders. He had lost an aunt and an uncle to the excesses of China's Cultural Revolution. He had seen families living in squalor, while local bureaucrats dined in splendour. Even a democratic country like Canada wasn't immune from abuses. Look at the injustices perpetrated on Japanese families during the Second World War, and the indignities suffered by Native peoples at the hands of the government in Ottawa for many years. A Cabinet minister had finally got around to apologizing for the mistakes of the past, but words were cheap compared with human suffering.

Things seemed to be better now, he acknowledged, but he still found the government overly intrusive. They made small business people like him and Mary into tax collectors; they demanded the completion of all kinds of complicated forms; and they took what seemed like an inordinate share of his income in the form of taxes.

So Henry had made it his business to find ways to alleviate the negative effects of big government on his small family. Nothing illegal, or even close to it, of course. The last thing he needed was trouble with tax collectors or bureaucratic clerks. But he knew from experience that there were always loopholes somewhere. It was a matter of searching them out.

His research into the Child Tax Benefit had got him thinking. If money from that source escaped the income-attribution rules, were there other exceptions as well? Ways in which cash could be put into baby Romney's name to be invested for her future education?

He started to dig, visiting the local library and poring through the books and documents there. He wished he could use the Internet; Jeff had told him it offered a wealth of information to those who could master its idiosyncracies and complexities. He would make it a point to learn about it at some stage, perhaps after the store was sold. But for now, he had to make do with the resources at hand. Still, they yielded a fair amount of information.

◆

The first thing Henry became aware of in his research was that the income-attribution rules applied only in cases where investment money was given to a child by a close relative. Any money that actually belonged to the child was not subject to the rules. However, it was a good idea to document the source of such money and keep the records, just in case Revenue Canada should ask questions in the future.

The possibilities he identified included the following:

Employment income. Any money earned by a child is legally hers. So the money could be invested on her behalf and any income earned would be considered to belong to the child for tax purposes.

Of course, employment opportunities for infants are rather slim, although Henry did think Romney was pretty enough for a television commercial, maybe sitting in a tire making goo-goo eyes at passing ducklings. But realistically, the chances were that she wouldn't be earning any money for many years. That was the whole purpose of this exercise; to keep her in school until she had gained at least a bachelor's degree.

But when she reached her teenage years, she might want to do some part-time work, perhaps in the summer. If times

PUT THE KIDS TO WORK
Any income actually earned by a minor child is considered his or hers for tax purposes, and can be invested without concern about the attribution rules.

were good and they still had a business at that stage, perhaps he and Mary could give her a job for a few hours each week. That would be money she could invest for college.

But there wouldn't be a lot. And she'd probably want to spend at least some of it. Plus, there would be very little time for any invested money to compound before she would be ready to go on to university.

It was an idea that might work for some families, he concluded, but not theirs.

Inheritances. If a child is the direct beneficiary of a will, any money received belongs to her and can be invested for future growth. Again, no attribution rules would apply.

Henry and Mary had a little money put aside, but not

IF SOMEONE DIES . . .
Inheritance money belongs to the recipient; this includes a child if the money is received directly and is not put in trust.

enough to make any real difference in Romney's case. In any event, they were both in good health and he hoped and expected they would be together for many more years, to watch Romney and any other grandchildren grow up.

There was no other possible source of an inheritance from their side. He doubted that Liz's mother was any better off.

Gifts from non-relatives. Financial gifts to a child from non-relatives, distant relatives, or from relatives living outside Canada are another potential source of investment money.

OUTSIDERS ARE EXEMPT
Gifts from non-relatives do not come under the attribution rules.

But the gifts must be legitimate, not a round-about way of directing money from a parent or grandparent through the hands of some outside person, in effect "laundering" it for tax purposes.

One important point that Henry learned in his reading was the importance of keeping any money that belonged to the child separate and distinct from all other funds, in its own account or investment plan. It should not be tainted in any way by mixing with other funds that would be subject to the attribution rules. Doing that would mess up everything.

◆

"So there are loopholes, just like I thought there would be," he reported to Mary with satisfaction. But then he added glumly, "The only problem is, they don't seem to help us very much. Other people might be able to use them, though."

"Maybe you should write a book about it," Mary said.

"Hmm," Henry replied. The idea had already occurred to him.

KEEP THE ACCOUNTS SEPARATE

Any money that is considered to be the child's for tax purposes (Child Tax Benefit, employment income, etc.) should be kept in a separate account or investment program. Mingling it with other funds may create tax problems in the future.

Chapter 9

Can You Trust "In-Trust"?

"*I* really hate going to the bank," Mary said. One of her responsibilities was to look after the deposits from their store. "The line-ups are always so long. You can wait forever, especially on Friday afternoons."

Henry looked up from the paper. He had been engrossed in an article on the impact of higher property taxes on small businesses when Mary's unexpected outburst came forth. It wasn't like her to complain, so he immediately paid attention even though the tax article was important to them.

"Well, then why don't you just use one of those automatic machines?"

Mary made a face. "Have you ever tried to figure them out? No, of course you haven't. And believe me, you don't want to. They seem to have a lot of problems. I saw a story just the other day about someone who made a deposit and the machine ate the money and didn't give a receipt. The person had a terrible time convincing the bank he'd ever had the cash.

"Anyway," she went on, "if I used the machine, I would never have learned the interesting piece of information I picked up today — something I think might be helpful in setting up that education plan you keep talking about for Romney."

"What? What is it?" Henry was all ears.

"It's something called an in-trust account. I heard the lady in front of me talking to the teller about it."

"You mean you eavesdropped?" Henry feigned shock.

"Not really. I mean, you can't help hearing when the line is so close. Anyway, the lady was saying her son had just received some money as a present and she wanted to open an account for him. The teller said it would be no problem, they had a special account for that purpose. I thought she called it an interest account, but when it was my turn I asked for more details. It's actually an in-trust account. The teller said it was the only way the bank could hold money for a child."

"That's very interesting," Henry said, the property-tax story completely gone from his mind. "I'm certainly going to have to investigate this."

◆

What Henry eventually learned is that informal in-trust accounts have become one of the most common ways of putting aside money for a child's college education. But he also discovered that there are a lot of grey areas and numerous potential pitfalls involved in going this route, which could result in some serious tax consequences.

In-trust accounts are easy to set up. Unfortunately, they are often set up improperly, exposing the parent or grandparent to potential problems down the road. And Revenue Canada can get tough if every T isn't properly crossed.

As an example of how tricky all this can be, let's look at a ruling RevCan issued on this subject in 1995. The department had received a letter from a father who wanted to set up an in-trust account for each of his two sons, to which he would contribute $100 a month for investment in an equity mutual fund. When the children came of legal age (eighteen or nineteen,

> **DANGER ZONE**
> *Many in-trust accounts are improperly set up, exposing the parents or grandparents to potential tax problems down the road. Putting the right structure in place is essential.*

depending on the province of residence), they would convert the assets to a personal account in their own names.

There was a caveat, however. The father noted that while this was his intent at the time, it was possible that a change in financial circumstances down the road would require him to encroach on the children's money for his own use.

He wanted to know the following from Revenue Canada:

1. Would an informal in-trust account such as he was contemplating constitute a "transfer of property" under the income-attribution rules?

2. If so, while first-generation interest and dividends would be attributed back to him, would capital gains be vested in the children for tax purposes?

3. What would be the tax consequences if he did have to encroach on the money later?

Here are the key portions of Revenue Canada's written response. This is the document that is currently being circulated to anyone who asks questions on this topic.

"1. It is our view that a 'transfer' will not take place. You have stated that the funds which accumulate in the 'in trust for' accounts may, depending on future circumstances, be used for purposes otherwise than for the sole benefit of your children and that you will have the right to withdraw funds... If the terms and conditions of the 'in trust for' accounts do not serve to divest, deprive or dispossess you of title to the deposited funds, then it may be concluded that a transfer of property has not been made. . . .

"2. [Since no transfer was made,] any income or loss from property, as well as any taxable capital gain or allowable capital loss from the disposition of the property, is attributed to the person from whom the property was directly or indirectly received if the terms of the trust are such that the property may revert to that person, may be distributed to the beneficiaries determined by that person at a time after the trust was created, or may only be disposed of with the consent of, or at the direction of, that person while alive."

Cutting through the legalese, what RevCan is essentially saying is that unless the money is irrevocably given to the children, the normal attribution rules do not apply and all investment profits, including capital gains, revert back to, in this case, the father for tax purposes. In other words, he might as well invest the money himself and forget about the in-trust accounts.

That's the last written word Revenue Canada had to offer on this subject at the time we were researching this book in the spring of 1998.

So, we asked, what does a parent have to do to ensure that a transfer actually does take place and the income-attribution rules can apply?

The verbal answer (which you won't find documented anywhere) is that the donor of the money and the person who manages it on the child's behalf (the trustee) must be two different people. A husband and wife were given as examples. Also, there must never be any encroachment on the invested money or the whole idea of an irrevocable trust will be blown right out of the water.

> **GIVE IT AWAY!**
> *Revenue Canada takes the view that if money is not given irrevocably to a child, no legal transfer has taken place. As a result, all dividends, interest, and capital gains are taxed in the hands of the donor.*

That's as close as we could get to an official government position on this issue. It would not be enough to satisfy a letter-of-the-law lawyer or a tax accountant. So be warned: even if you follow these guidelines to the letter, there is no guarantee you won't have problems later, especially if a large amount of money is involved.

Still, so many people are operating on this basis, often with the encouragement and guidance of professionals, that it seems hard to believe the government would suddenly decide to shift gears and begin reassessing taxpayers on the basis of in-trust accounts that were set up according to the guidelines. So let's look at the rules more closely.

Basically, an in-trust account requires three participants: a beneficiary, in this case the child; a donor, who is the person who is putting up the money; and a trustee, who has the responsibility for managing the assets in the account. Remember that the donor and the trustee must not be the same person, otherwise the trust may be voided, with unhappy tax consequences for all concerned.

If the in-trust account is being set up by the parents (the

THREE PARTICIPANTS

In-trust accounts require three participants: a beneficiary (the child), a donor (the person who puts up the money), and a trustee (the person who administers the funds). It is important that the donor and the trustee not be the same person.

most common example), one of them will take on the role of donor while the other acts as the trustee. The problem is that most people in the bank or brokerage firm where the account is being set up don't understand this important distinction and may not tell you about it. Most financial institutions don't have any special form or instruction sheet on how to proceed (although some say they're working on it). There are some exceptions, however. Trimark Mutual Funds is one. They have developed a special form for setting up in-trust accounts, along the guidelines suggested by Revenue Canada. It clearly identifies the various participants and their respective roles. The forms are supplied to investment dealers who offer Trimark products. Some other fund companies are now doing the same.

Our advice is to set up your in-trust account with a financial institution or investment firm that does have a special form for situations of this type, a form that follows the verbal rules outlined by Revenue Canada. This isn't a guarantee that you will never be challenged, but it should certainly help your case.

The bottom line is that it's up to you to ensure it's all done properly. That means having the appropriate documentation, which clearly spells out the relationships, just in case you're ever questioned.

Once a proper in-trust account is set up, any assets contributed to it may be invested at the discretion of the trustee. Here's where the advantage of this type of account comes into play. Let's create a situation to illustrate. We'll say a young couple sets up an in-trust account for their infant son, Robert, with the idea of using it to save for college. The mother takes the role of donor, putting up the initial cash. The father becomes the trustee.

As we've already learned, under the income-attribution rules any first-generation dividends or interest payments are attributed back to the mother for tax purposes. The fact that this is a trust account doesn't change that. But all capital gains earned in the account are considered to belong to the son for tax purposes (we'll assume that Revenue Canada will agree that a "transfer" of money has occurred in this case). This creates an income-splitting situation that can be used to build a very large education fund.

Let's say the mother, as donor, contributes $1,000 every year to the account for eighteen years. The father, as trustee, invests the money on Robert's behalf. He has a wide range of choices available. An in-trust account isn't limited to bank deposits by any means. It can be used to buy Canada Savings Bonds, purchase mutual funds, or set up an investment portfolio.

Keeping the attribution rules in mind, Dad decides to invest the money in equity mutual funds that pay mainly capital-gains distributions. He chooses his funds well, and over time the in-trust account grows by an average of 12 percent annually. At the end of the eighteenth year, the account is worth — hold on now — almost $56,000.

That could create a large tax bill for son Robert when it comes time to draw out those gains. But Dad has been smart. Along the way, acting in his role as trustee, he has periodically sold some mutual-fund units and reinvested the money elsewhere. In doing so, he has crystallized some of the capital gains for tax purposes. Whenever this has been done, a tax return has been prepared for young Robert (yes, children need to file tax returns if they have adequate income) and the capital gains declared. Dad has been careful to always keep the taxable gains to less than $8,600 in any given year. Since only 75 percent of gains are taxable (the rest is free), an $8,600 capital gain works out to $6,450 in taxable income. As long as baby Robert has no other income, that amount can be offset by the personal tax credit, so the tax payable is zero.

By carefully managing the money in this way over the years, Dad has been able to build Robert a $56,000 tax-free nest egg, which Mom and Dad hope will be enough to allow their pride and joy to earn his degree in computer science. If all goes well, that's exactly what will happen. But family

CRYSTALLIZING GAINS
Taking some capital gains along the way can reduce or even eliminate the tax burden when money is drawn out to attend college. This is one of the administrative responsibilities of the plan's trustee.

relationships are not always so neat and predictable.

The potential problem here is that the money in the in-trust account belongs irrevocably to the child. That's a key condition for making the whole process work. So as the contributing parent (or grandparent), you can no longer consider it yours to dip into whenever the need arises. This applies not only to the income earned in the trust, but also to the capital you originally contributed. Legally, it's gone. The trustee may decide how the money is to be invested, but it is the child's property.

Think about this carefully before you set up such an account. It means that when the child turns eighteen and legally becomes an adult, at least as far as Revenue Canada is concerned, all the money in the account belongs to him or her. You may have intended it as an education fund, but there is no legal way you can insist the money be used for that purpose. If your son decides to use it to fly off to Europe, to buy a set of wheels, or heaven forbid, to get into drugs, you can't stop him. It's his money.

That stops a lot of parents cold when they consider the implications. There might conceivably be a lot of money

IT'S THEIR MONEY
When children reach the age of majority, any money held in an in-trust account automatically becomes their property. The parents have no claim to the cash. So if the kids decide to fly off to Nepal instead of going to college with the money, they can.

involved when the youngster comes of age. And there's no way of knowing what the cute baby of today will be like eighteen years down the road. A rebellious teen with thousands of dollars suddenly at his disposal is not a pleasant thought to contemplate.

Of course, there's nothing that says you have to tell the child that the fund exists. But the trust will dissolve when the child comes of age, and the bank, brokerage firm, or mutual-fund company holding the money will probably start sending statements directly to the beneficiary once the eighteenth birthday has passed. So it may be tough to keep it a secret.

Here again, however, things may not always be as they seem — another example of the dense fog that continues to surround this whole area.

Trimark, which has studied this issue in great depth, believes it is on sound legal ground with a policy that amounts to something like "Yes, it's yours, but you can't have it." Their bulletin, entitled "In-Trust Accounts," contains the following statement: "When the child reaches the age of majority . . . he or she takes control of the funds. Beneficial ownership of the account has always resided with the child, and although the trustee has managed the money, the informal trust dissolves when the beneficiary reaches the age of majority. Trimark, however, will not give the child access to the funds automatically — we will await instructions from the trustee."

Come again? There is no trust any more and the child, now an adult, has taken control of the funds, but Trimark won't give them the money?

Trimark says their view is that while the child is the "beneficial owner" of the assets, the trustee is the "legal owner." Therefore, the assets cannot be released without the trustee's consent.

It sounds reassuring to parents. However, how it would all play out if the trustee refused to release the money and the child sued is an interesting question. No one has the answer to that at this stage, although Willson McTavish, the Children's Lawyer for the Province of Ontario, says that if the issue ever came across his desk, there is no question who his office would side with — the child. "Being a trustee is the highest duty known to law," he observes. "The parents must be impeccable in this regard."

There's another angle that might be worth exploring: loaning money to your child or grandchild in trust, rather than gifting it. In this case, you would at least retain control over the capital if the child decided to use the money for some undesirable purpose upon attaining adulthood.

The problem with this approach is that there have been

all kinds of unanswered questions surrounding it and, until recently, no one had ever put it to the test.

Revenue Canada actually contemplates this possibility in its Interpretation Bulletin IT-510. In it, RevCan states that the attribution rules apply "where an individual has transferred or loaned property (including money) to a related minor or to a trust in which a related minor is beneficially interested." So according to their rules, there appears to be no reason why you could not loan money, rather than give it, to an informal trust set up for your child, thereby retaining the legal right to require repayment of the principal.

But hold on a minute. Revenue Canada also takes the position that for the attribution rule that excludes capital gains to apply, the loan must be "genuine." However, lawyers we talked to on this issue said it was not possible for a minor child to sign an enforceable loan agreement. In fact, if the child is still an infant, it would not be possible for it to sign anything at all, much less understand what the whole issue is about. We were faced with something of a catch-22: according to Revenue Canada, loans to minors look okay, but there didn't seem any obvious way to do it.

So we requested a formal ruling from Revenue Canada. We received a response in July 1998 and the answers indicate that it may be relatively safe to use a loan for this purpose.

In fact, properly applied, Revenue Canada's ruling sets up a sort of have-your-cake-and-eat-it-too scenario which would allow a parent or grandparent to protect some of the assets in an in-trust account from misuse by a child who chooses not to go on to university.

The questions we posed to RevCan were as follows:

1. What attribution rules would apply in the case of a loan to a trust?
2. What is a "genuine" loan?
3. Would interest have to be charged?
4. Could the principal be repaid at the age of majority?

In the response, Revenue Canada affirms that if a parent (or by extension a grandparent) makes a genuine loan to a trust for a minor child, any capital gains earned as a result of investments made with the capital will indeed be considered to belong to the child for tax purposes.

In reaching this conclusion, RevCan states that for capital gains to be attributed back to the donor (something you absolutely do not want to happen), the terms of the trust would have to be "such that the property . . . may revert to that person, be distributed to beneficiaries determined by that person at a time after the trust was created, or only be disposed of with the consent of, or at the discretion of, that person while alive."

In other words, you will foul things up if you try to reclaim the money given to a trust, change the beneficiaries after it has been set up, or try to exercise control over how the assets are used.

But doesn't a loan amount to reclaiming the money? No, the ruling goes on to say. "A genuine loan to a trust would not by itself be considered to result in property being held by the trust under one or more of these conditions . . . if the loan is outside and independent of the terms of the trust."

The ruling then goes on to refer to paragraph 3 of Interpretation Bulletin IT-260, quoting as follows:

"No all-inclusive statement can be made as to when a loan can be considered to be 'genuine,' but a written and signed acknowledgment of the loan by the borrower and agreement to repay it within a reasonable period of time ordinarily is accepted evidence that it was so. If, in addition, there is evidence that the borrower has given security for the loan, that interest on the loan has been paid, or that actual repayment has been made, it is accepted that the loan is genuine. The fact that no interest is required to be paid does not mean, in itself, that a genuine loan has not been made."

Okay, so now we know it can be an interest-free loan without endangering the capital gains belonging to the child. But how can your two-year-old daughter sign the document that makes it genuine?

As it turns out, she doesn't have to. In fact, Revenue Canada states flatly that whether the child can sign or not is "not relevant if the loan is made to a trust, as the trustee of the trust would be the person signing the loan agreement on the trust's behalf."

There's the key to the magic formula. As we've already explained, there must be three parties to a trust: the beneficiary, the trustee, and the donor (settlor). It is absolutely essential in setting up an informal in-trust account that all three roles be filled by different people.

For example, Jim Jones may decide to set up an in-trust account for year-old son Brian, loaning the trust $10,000 as seed capital. Jim asks his wife, Sue, to be the trustee and she agrees. Sue therefore enters into the loan agreement on the trust's behalf, in her role as trustee. Young Brian signs nothing (as if he could!) and owes nothing. The debt is incurred by the trust.

Now comes the final piece in the puzzle — repayment. One of Revenue Canada's criteria for a "genuine" loan is repayment within a reasonable period of time. What's that? Here the ruling is fuzzy:

"The determination of what is a 'reasonable period of time' would be based on the facts of a particular case and we cannot advise that repayment only after the child reaching the age of majority is reasonable," they state.

In other words, be careful with the repayment terms of the loan. Revenue Canada has served notice that if you allow too long a time to elapse before repayment, they could challenge the legitimacy of the loan and reassess, applying the capital gains to the donor.

So build a repayment schedule into the loan agreement. You may want to structure it so that repayments in the early years are relatively small, thus maximizing the returns from the invested capital. As the value of the trust builds, the repayments can increase.

There are no clear guidelines as to what time-frame will be acceptable. But if a schedule is put into place at the time of the loan and is adhered to, it seems unlikely you'll run into problems on the basis of this ruling.

The advantage of this approach is that it allows you to get more money into an education savings program early, assuming the capital is available. The capital gains are earned by the child and tax sheltered by using the personal tax credit. Plus you are able to recover your original money from the trust, thereby ensuring that the whole amount of principal and capital gains is not exposed to misuse when the child turns eighteen.

Another alternative is to set up a formal trust, with specific conditions attached. Any trust company can do this for you. The end result will be a lot more certainty, but this is a much more expensive route to go.

A plan of this type is known technically as an *inter vivos* trust. That simply means it is a trust that has been set up by a living person, not as a condition of a will after death. The person whose money is used to set up the trust is known as the settlor. As is the case with an in-trust account, the person who will draw on the assets is the beneficiary. The responsibility for acting as trustee is usually assumed by a trust company, although that doesn't have to be the case.

A formal trust can be "discretionary" or "non-discretionary." A non-discretionary trust means the beneficiary can do whatever he or she wants with the money. Since you're going to the trouble and expense of doing all this to avoid exactly that situation, this isn't the way you want to go.

Instead, you set up a discretionary trust, spelling out the specific terms and conditions for which the money is to be used. You may, for example, state that the assets (capital and income) can be used only for education purposes until such time as the beneficiary turns twenty-five. After that, you might allow the money to be used for some other reason, for example, to buy a home. The point is that you retain some control over how the money can be used, which you cannot do with an informal in-trust account.

There are some other advantages to setting up a formal trust, beyond retaining some control over the use of the money. For one, there is no age limitation to consider. The trust doesn't turn into a pumpkin when the beneficiary blows out eighteen (or nineteen) candles on his cake.

Income-attribution rules apply to a formal trust in exactly the same way as they do to a properly structured informal in-trust account. First-generation dividends and interest are taxable in the hands of the settlor as long as the child is a minor, while capital gains are not.

The major disadvantage is cost. To set up such a trust will set you back $1,000 or more initially. As well, there will be annual trustee fees, usually based on a percentage of the assets in the trust. Get quotes from a trust company before proceeding.

FORMAL TRUSTS ARE EXPENSIVE
A formal trust gives a parent more control over how the money is eventually used. But the costs are high. You'll pay an initial set-up fee, plus annual charges. The whole package can run to several thousand dollars.

The bottom line is that, in practical terms, this option is really available only to the well-off.

There are also some special tax considerations that apply to a formal trust, such as a deemed disposition of the assets every twenty-one years for tax purposes. For taxation purposes, a deemed disposition is considered to be the same thing as a sale, so all capital gains in the portfolio would become taxable at that time. You'll want to get all the details from a trust company representative before proceeding in this way.

With both formal and informal trusts, there are no contribution limits or investment restrictions. This is an important consideration for parents of older children or for a family that wants to invest a considerable amount of money up front in an education program. The reason is that the government limits annual contributions to a registered education savings plan (RESP) to $4,000. This makes it very difficult to build a large RESP fund for a child who is already in his or her teens, and severely penalizes parents who were late in starting. By using a trust, this restriction is eliminated.

◆

"What's this, Dad?" Jeff asked as Henry pushed the piece of paper across the table after Sunday dinner.

"Just a little something for Romney. Your mother and I set up an in-trust account for her this week. We've put some money in a mutual fund. It's not a lot, just $100 for now. But it will get her started and we'll add more whenever we can."

Jeff knew how tight things were for his parents, and the sacrifice this meant. "Thank you both," he said. The affection in his voice was unmistakable.

"You're welcome. We just ask one thing of you and Liz."

"Anything."

"Just make sure that Romney grows up to be a fine, responsible person so that the money will be used properly."

"We'll do our best, Dad. We truly will."

Chapter 10

The Evolution of RESPs

*H*enry had to admit he was impressed. He did so reluctantly, of course, given his lifelong aversion to governments. But you have to give the devil his due, he thought as he read the report in *The Globe and Mail.* Ottawa was finally going to do something to help young people get the kind of education they need. And just in time to benefit little Romney, too.

He scanned through the details again. The finance minister, Paul Martin, had told the House of Commons in his budget speech of February 24, 1998, that the government was setting up a new grant system to supplement the money contributed by parents and grandparents to registered education savings plans — RESPs, as they are known.

Henry had done some research into RESPs, but in the end he had been left somewhat sceptical about them. This new government program might force him to change his view, however. He went to the kitchen for some scissors to clip out the article. The family would need to have a full discussion about this.

◆

RESPs have been around for many years. However, they didn't attract a lot of interest from Canadian parents until the mid-1990s, when university tuition fees began to skyrocket and articles started appearing in the newspapers about the heavy student-loan debt loads many graduates had incurred by the time they received a degree.

An RESP is a government-approved tax shelter specifically designed for education savings. However, despite the similarity in name, it operates quite differently from its cousin, the registered retirement savings plan (RRSP).

For example, contributions to an RESP are not tax-deductible. Any money that goes into the plan is contributed on an after-tax basis. Once in the RESP, however, any future investment income that is earned remains tax-sheltered until it is withdrawn.

NO DEDUCTION
Unlike an RRSP, there is no tax deduction for contributing to a registered education savings plan. That may explain why they have never caught on with the Canadian public.

An RESP may be set up for a child at any time. The maximum annual contribution is $4,000 per child. You can contribute for up to twenty-one years, but the total cumulative amount of the contributions cannot exceed $42,000 per beneficiary. Unlike an RRSP, unused contribution room cannot be carried forward.

Plans mature twenty-five years after they are set up (too soon, in our opinion). If the money has not been used for education purposes by that time, special rules come into play, which we'll get to later.

As long as the RESP contract permits it (and this is an important point to verify before signing up for a plan), capital contributions may be withdrawn any time tax-free. So if, for example, a mother contributes $20,000 to an RESP over several years and then needs the money, she can take out that amount without any tax consequences. The reason this is possible is that there was no tax deduction given at the time the cash went into the plan originally.

Any income earned within the plan will be taxable when it is withdrawn. However, it's the student, not the subscriber (parent, grandparent, etc.), who will be on the hook. Since most students have very little income and can claim tuition and education credits, the tax liability may be non-existent.

We say "may be" because it all depends on how much is in the plan and how much is taken out each year. Suppose, for example, an RESP is opened in the first year of a daughter's life and the parents contribute $2,000 a year to it for the next twenty years. The money is invested wisely and earns an average annual compound rate of return of 9 percent. Now she is twenty years old and ready for college. The parents check their RESP statement and discover to their delight that the plan is worth a little more than $102,000! Wonderful!

The next move is to minimize the taxes that will be payable on that money when it comes out of the RESP. As a first step, the plan's contributor makes a tax-free withdrawal of the $40,000 that have been invested in the RESP over the years. That will leave about $62,000 for education spending.

Ideally, all the money in an RESP should be used for this purpose. If there are still funds in the plan when it matures after twenty-five years (the maximum life of an RESP), they could be taxed at an extremely high rate, as we'll explain later in this chapter.

Let's look at an example. Suppose the daughter decides to take a three-year B.A. To use all the money in this plan, she would have to spend about $21,000 a year (actually a little more since the balance left in the RESP would continue to earn more income each year). In all probability, she'll end up paying some tax on that money, perhaps as much as $3,000 to $4,000. So don't expect that every cent that comes out of an RESP will be tax-free. It won't happen that way in many cases.

Interestingly, although the Income Tax Act says the proceeds from an RESP must be used for education, there are no hard and fast rules as to what this actually covers. You can't get a pamphlet from the federal government telling you what the money can or cannot be spent on, since no regulations have ever been put into place. The Department of Finance has been very loosey-goosey on this one. Generally speaking, education payments include tuition fees, books, equipment, lab fees, student fees, sports fees, accommodation, and transportation. However, if the student is in full-time attendance at an approved post-secondary institution, the government doesn't require any receipts or other evidence of how the money is spent. (Of course, if fraud was suspected they could always sic Revenue Canada on you to investigate.)

So a lot is open to personal interpretation. For example, there is no reason why a full-time student living at home could not direct some of his RESP money to his parents for room and board. That could be worth several thousand dollars a year and is an excellent strategy for getting money out of a plan, while still keeping it in the family. If they wished, and could afford it, the parents could put the money aside and gift it back to their child as a graduation present.

> **FEW RESTRICTIONS**
> *There are no hard and fast rules on how the money from an RESP must be spent. As long as you can show that it was in some way connected with education (even if the connection is somewhat tenuous), you probably won't have any problems.*

There are many other possibilities to consider. For example, we asked a finance department official if a beneficiary could decide to study at a university in Europe. Could plane fare, living expenses, and all the rest qualify as an "education" payment for RESP purposes? The answer was yes.

So you can use an RESP to send your son or daughter to the Sorbonne, the London School of Economics, Harvard, or MIT. It may be a Canadian program, but there is no geographic limitation on how the money can be used.

That raises the issue of which institutions qualify for payments under an RESP, and here you must be careful. The government's definition is quite broad and includes Canadian universities, community colleges, CEGEP, junior colleges, and technical schools. Universities outside Canada also qualify, as do some correspondence courses and certain other post-secondary institutions.

However, you must check with the sponsor of the specific RESP you are considering to see if they allow this broad latitude. We have been informed of cases where parents were not given access to RESP funds they had accumulated because the child attended a school that wasn't recognized by the specific plan, even though it fell within government guidelines. As a result, they lost thousands of dollars. Some of the older programs offered by the pooled plans are quite restrictive in this regard (see Chapter 11).

Even within the same RESP sponsor, some plan options may carry different rules relating to the eligibility of an educational institution. So be very careful. Most parents want the maximum possible flexibility.

There are no governmental restrictions on the level of degree for which an RESP may be used (although here again individual plans may vary). Your child could, in theory at least, go all the way through medical school on RESP funding. However, this is an example of how the twenty-five-year limit on the life of an RESP can be a problem. If the student wishes to take medicine or law or an advanced program of graduate studies, the clock may tick down too soon and force the premature withdrawal of needed funds. We recommend that the government consider extending the deadline if a student is actively attending classes. But unless that happens, all studies must be completed within the allotted time frame.

> **CHECK THE RULES**
>
> *Some RESP companies have different rules on school eligibility, depending on which of their plans you select. Make sure you fully understand the choices before signing up.*

The 1998 federal budget introduced a new program that is intended to make RESP saving even more attractive for parents and grandparents. It's called the Canada Education Savings Grant (CESG) and it amounts to a government subsidy to your own savings.

The federal government will add an extra 20 percent to your annual RESP contribution each year, up to a maximum of $400 annually. (The administrator of the RESP will apply for the grant on your child's behalf.) So you need to put at least $2,000 into the plan each year to qualify for the maximum payment. The maximum lifetime grant per child is $7,200. That's $400 a year for eighteen years.

The grant will be paid directly into the RESP, not to you or the child personally. Children are eligible for it up to age seventeen. However, in the case of teens aged sixteen and seventeen, a grant will be paid only if there have been contributions to the plan of at least $300 a year for a minimum of four years before the child turned sixteen, or if total previous contributions had reached $4,000 before that time. The idea here appears to be to discourage people from setting up a last-minute RESP just to get a grant.

Since the grant limit is $400 a year, you won't get credit for a contribution in any given year that is in excess of $2,000, even though you're allowed to put up to $4,000 into the plan. However, you can carry forward unused grant room. For example, suppose you contribute $500 to an RESP this year, earning a CESG of $100 (20 percent x $500). You have unused CESG room of $300 ($400 - $100 claimed), which you can carry forward to next year or beyond. So you could contribute $3,500 to the RESP next year and earn a grant of $700 ($400 for the current year plus the $300 carry-forward credit). Yes, it sounds complicated, but the money can add up.

The addition of the CESG changes the math for RESPs considerably. Here's an example: Suppose you set up a plan under the old rules in the year your child was born and contributed $2,000 a year to it for eighteen years. Your total contribution is $36,000. Let's say you invested the money in conservative mutual funds and generated an average annual return of 8 percent over that time. At the end of the day, the RESP would be worth a total of $74,900.

Now let's make the same assumptions but factor in the CESG at a rate of $400 a year. That's additional capital of $7,200 for the plan. With this hefty bonus, the total value at the end works out to $89,880. The annual return on your personal invested capital has shot up to almost 9.9 percent. In effect, the government has made your child a gift of about $15,000 to help pay the costs of higher education. Very generous of them!

That is, if the child or an alternate beneficiary chooses to make use of it. (Whether you can switch to an alternate will depend on the terms of your RESP contract. For purposes of the CESG, only siblings are acceptable alternates.) If not, the trustees of

HEALTHY BONUS
Depending on how the money is invested, the new Canada Education Savings Grants could add $15,000 or more to the value of your child's college fund when accumulated interest is taken into account.

your RESP have a responsibility to ensure that Ottawa gets its money back, with interest. That's correct. If the child does not go on to college or university, the government will take back the total accumulated grant, plus any income that money may have earned inside the plan over the years. So in some cases, we'll see the Great Disappearing Act. The money that was there, won't be.

This brings us to the proverbial fly in the ointment. There is a financial danger in using an RESP for education saving. We have not been able to quantify it — no one seems to have the appropriate statistics — but it does exist and you must take it into account before setting up a plan.

The problem arises if the child does not go on to post-secondary studies and there is no one else that can be substituted as a beneficiary. In this situation, all the accumulated income is at risk. The original capital can be withdrawn, because it was paid with after-tax dollars. But the earnings are another matter. You risk having part or all of that money taken from you.

The Income Tax Act stipulates that the earnings inside an RESP must be used for education purposes. Although, as we have seen, that can be defined very broadly, the fact is that the plan beneficiary must take some post-secondary studies to make use of the money.

Until 1997, any RESP earnings that could not be used by a family for post-secondary study were forfeited — literally. That's what happened in the case of co-author Frank Jones. Depending on the terms of the specific RESP, the money either went to provide financial assistance to other students or was donated to an educational institution of the family's choice.

The other co-author of this book focused national attention on the problem in a series of CBC Radio financial commentaries that aired in April 1996. In them, he called RESPs a form of "education roulette" and said that unsuspecting families could lose tens of thousands of dollars in investment income as a result of these rules.

He suggested the government change the law to allow RESP-earned income not used for education to be withdrawn as a lump sum by the beneficiary when the plan matures, to be taxed at his or her marginal rate — much the same principle as is used for lump-sum RRSP withdrawals. The government would end up collecting tax on the investment income at a rate of 40 to 50 percent in most cases, which is fair enough considering the income was tax sheltered over many years.

The broadcasts drew a lot of public reaction, pro and con. Some players in the RESP industry were upset because they felt people would be unduly alarmed by them.

Perhaps it was just coincidence, but in the 1997 federal budget, Paul Martin acknowledged that the problem really existed and introduced two alternatives to try to deal with it. The first allowed for a tax-free transfer of the accumulated earnings into an RRSP. This could be done only by the original contributor to the plan, not the beneficiary. The catch is that the maximum amount that can be switched in this way was set at $40,000 (to be moved up to $50,000 in 1999), and the contributor must have the RRSP contribution room available.

Alternatively, the money could be withdrawn from the RESP for personal use, again by the original contributor only. However, in this case the withdrawal will be treated as income in the year it is received and will be subject to a 20 percent penalty over and above the applicable tax rate. In many cases, this means the amount of money taken from the RESP will push the contributor into the top tax bracket. When the penalty tax is added on, the effective rate for people in most parts of the country will be between 65 and 75 percent.

Going back to our illustration, let's suppose the RRSP room is not available and this becomes the only option. As the contributor, you'll be able to take your original capital of $36,000 tax-free. The CESG portion, with interest, is repaid to the government by the plan administrator. The other $38,900, which represents income earned over the years, will be taxed at the special rate. If you have other income, the RESP amount will be taxed on top of your regular earnings.

STILL A RISK
Thanks to recent budget changes, there are now ways to get back your investment earnings from an RESP if the child does not go on to college. But the rules are still unnecessarily restrictive. Families may lose heavily if a child is not college material.

So there's a good possibility that you'll end up paying tax on the money at the top rate. Let's say that comes in at 70 percent in your province. You will get to keep only $11,670. The rest goes to Ottawa. That works out to an annual return of only 3.2 percent on your invested capital. That's the risk you face, using the RESP formula.

There are two ways to reduce the tax impact, however. The first is to declare both spouses as co-contributors when the RESP is set up. This was made possible as a result of the 1997 budget, and can have important implications if money has to be withdrawn in the future because it cannot be used for education purposes or transferred to an RRSP. This approach allows a couple to split the money withdrawn from a plan between them — which may result in a reduced tax rate. However, the co-contributor designation can only be done at the time a plan is set up, not years later.

The second tax-saving technique is to spread the withdrawal of the RESP money over two years. This is permitted under the Income Tax Act; if any "accumulated income payment" is taken from an RESP for non-education purposes, the balance must come out by March 31 of the year following.

Going back to our illustration, this would allow for a withdrawal of $19,450 (half of $38,900) in year one and the rest in year two. If the co-contributor rule could be applied, each spouse would be taxed on $9,725 in each year. This could reduce the tax payable considerably, depending on their other income.

It's important to note that several conditions must be met before any money can be withdrawn from an RESP using either of these options. The plan must have been in existence for at least ten years, all the beneficiaries must be at least twenty-one years old and not pursuing higher education, and the contributor must be a resident of Canada. If any of these conditions are not met, then the earned income in the plan will be forfeited.

There are other factors to consider when deciding whether an RESP is the best choice for education savings. For example, an RESP limits the annual contribution to $4,000. However, an education plan will grow more effectively if a larger amount can be invested at an early age. Let's say a parent or grandparent has a lump sum of $25,000 available to invest when a child is born. A non-RESP in-trust account is set up with the money. We'll again assume 8 percent annual growth and say that not one more penny is put towards this purpose for the next eighteen years. At the end of that time, the plan contains $99,900. You've invested $11,000 less in capital than with the RESP example we looked at, but you have $10,000 more than would be the case with the $2,000 annual contributions, even with the CESG included.

Ah, but what about the effect of taxes, you ask, since this must be done outside an RESP? There's the rub; however, it can be dealt with. You'll recall that while interest and dividends are attributed back to the parent or grandparent, capital gains are not. They belong to the child for whom you have set up this trust. If you invest in stocks or mutual funds that pay mainly or exclusively capital gains, the tax effect can be minimized or eliminated. However, some management is required, since the capital gains will need to be crystallized periodically to ensure the child doesn't face a huge tax bill when the money is drawn upon.

The virtue of this approach is that the money is not subject to a government clawback if a child does not proceed to post-secondary study. It can be used for other purposes.

It's unfortunate that people have to make these tough decisions in what amounts to a vacuum. Who knows what your infant daughter may choose to do when she hits her high-school and college years?

One way to reduce the risk, which many RESP promoters have introduced, is to set up a family plan if you have more than one child. It will cover all the children in your family, so if one decides not to go on to college, the others can benefit from the extra money. This at least provides a measure of protection against having the government snatch most of it back twenty years or so down the road. However, the twenty-five-year maturity rule can pose a real problem for younger children, who may not have adequate time to complete their university studies before the RESP must be wound up.

There are a number of other rules governing RESPs that

> **IMPROVING THE ODDS**
>
> *Family plans improve the chances that RESP earnings will be used by at least one of your children. But the time limits on them may leave the youngest siblings short-changed.*

you should be aware of if you're considering a plan. These are government requirements; individual RESPs may impose additional restrictions.

Short-term studies. Some RESP promoters have made much of the fact that if a child chooses not to go on to college, a parent can designate him- or herself as the plan beneficiary and use the money to take short-term courses. This is indeed allowed, but the 1998 budget limited the amount that could be withdrawn from an RESP for courses of less than three months to the cost of tuition plus $300 a week. Application can be made to Human Resources Canada to have the $300 limit increased, but you'd need to supply a good reason. This restriction appears to be designed to clamp down on the idea of using RESP money to take three-week art courses in Bali or on the Riviera.

Time limit on contributions. Although an RESP does not have to be terminated until December 31 of the year the plan reaches its twenty-fifth anniversary, contributions are permitted for only the first twenty-one years.

Repayment of CESG. There are other circumstances under which the Canada Education Savings Grant would have to be repaid to the government besides a child not going on to post-secondary studies. They include:

1. When an RESP is terminated or revoked.
2. When income is taken from an RESP for non-educational purposes.
3. When a plan beneficiary is replaced, unless the new beneficiary is under twenty-one and is either a brother or a sister, or both beneficiaries are related to the subscriber by blood or adoption.
4. When there is a transfer to another RESP that involves either a change in beneficiary or a partial transfer of funds.

Taxation. Payments from an RESP to a student are called education assistance payments (EAP). They are taxable in the student's hands as "other income." Students should receive a T4A Supplementary slip from the company that administers the RESP reporting such payments.

Overcontributions. If you put too much money into an RESP (remember the maximum is $4,000 a year to a lifetime limit of $42,000 per beneficiary), you'll be hit with a penalty tax on the excess. It amounts to one percent a month on the extra money and is payable until the overcontribution is withdrawn.

Time limit. RESP contributions must be made by December 31 of any year. Note that this is a different deadline than that which applies to RRSPs.

The amount of money that can accumulate in an RESP account over time can be significant. But it will vary considerably, depending on the investment strategy you select. Let's look at some options. In all cases, we'll use an average annual compound rate of return of 8 percent and assume a time frame of eighteen years. We will also assume the child is eligible for the CESG payments.

Scenario One

You save $1,200 annually ($100 a month) for eighteen years. The government grant amounts to $240 a year.

Total personal capital invested	$21,600
Value of CESG	4,320
Income earned over eighteen years	28,008
Final value of plan	53,928

Scenario Two

You save $2,333.33 annually ($194.44 a month) for eighteen years, thus obtaining the maximum possible government grant of $400 a year.

Total personal capital invested	$42,000
Value of CESG	7,200
Income earned over eighteen years	53,164
Final value of plan	102,364

Scenario Three

You save $4,000 annually ($333.33 a month) for ten years and add another $2,000 in year eleven. This brings you to $42,000, the maximum amount you may invest in an RESP on behalf of any one child. The government grant amounts to $400 a year for eleven years, the maximum allowed. After that, you make no contributions and get no more CESG.

Total personal capital invested	$42,000
Value of CESG	4,400
Income earned over eighteen years	75,693
Final value of plan	122,093

Take a close look at the last scenario. This involves front-end loading the RESP to the maximum extent allowed by law. By doing so, you forgo a considerable amount of the CESG (you'll leave $2,800 on the table). Despite this, the total value of the RESP at the end of the day is worth considerably more than in scenario two, in which you put up the same amount of capital and maximized the government grant. The difference is that in scenario three, you are making maximum use of the time value of money. The CESG is not enough to overcome that.

◆

"Why must they make it so complicated?" Henry complained. "Here they go and do a good thing by helping people save for a child's education — and you know how hard it is for me to admit governments can do anything good," he said, grinning at Jeff and Liz. "But then they turn around and put in all these conditions and crazy rules. Can you imagine losing all that money if little Romney doesn't want to go to college? Of course she will, but some people's children — well, they won't, we know that. So what does the government think it's gaining by putting families at risk like that?"

Jeff shrugged. He was amused at his father's tirade, but at the same time he knew the older man was making an important point.

"They should be doing everything they can to encourage

young people to save for their children," Henry went on. "After all, it will save them millions in tax dollars in future years. So why the barriers, why the uncertainty?"

"Okay, Dad, suppose you were running things. What would you do?"

"That's easy," Henry said. He'd been doing a lot of reading on this subject. "First, I would take away the $4,000 annual limit. If people have more money to put aside for their kids or grandchildren, let them. Keep the total limit if you like, but get rid of this annual thing.

"Then I would put rules in place for taking out the money if the child doesn't go to college — rules that don't end up confiscating almost everything. After all, kids have other needs. Let them do the same as with RRSPs: use the money to buy a house or something. It's not so hard. Damn politicians!"

Jeff nodded. His dad may not have had a lot of education, but he sure had more than his share of common sense.

Chapter 11

The RESP Jungle

"What a mess!" Mary threw up her hands in frustration at the sight of her kitchen table buried beneath piles of documents. She had just come upstairs from the shop, where she had spent the last three hours training a new clerk. When she'd left, the table had been in its usual tidy state. "What is all this, Henry? What are you doing? It's almost time for dinner, you have to clean all this up."

Henry was seated in the midst of all the papers, his head in his hands. He hadn't even heard Mary come in, so absorbed was he in the material before him. Wearily, he looked up.

"It's all education stuff," he explained. "For Romney. I sent away for information on some of these RESPs I've been telling you about. It all arrived in the afternoon mail, just after you left. I've been trying to make some sense out of it ever since."

He pushed the colourful pamphlets and booklets around. There were pictures of smiling families holding babies, of graduation ceremonies, of fulfilled-looking young adults in lab coats and pilot uniforms. "Your hopes, their dreams," one pamphlet read. "Building the dream together," said another. "Secure the future," urged a third. "Will your child be able to afford college?" asked a fourth.

"I've been reading through this stuff all afternoon," Henry said. "I'm more confused now than when I started. So many types of plans. So many options. So many what-ifs. I don't know if these things are a good idea or not."

Mary's face softened. Henry had been working so hard on this, it was impossible to be angry with him, even if the table was a mess.

"You just need some time to think about all you've read and to digest it," she said softly. "Pick up all this stuff and put it away for now. You'll feel better when you've had something to eat. I've got some nice fresh scallops; we'll have them in a stir-fry."

Henry brightened. He loved scallops. "I'll have it all cleaned up in no time," he promised.

◆

Henry isn't alone. The RESP can be extremely confusing. After weighing all the pros and cons, parents have to decide if the concept is right for them. If they do come to the conclusion it's a good idea, they then have to decide what type of plan to select.

Essentially, there are two basic types of RESPs, although there are many variables within the two categories. Let's look at each.

Pooled Plans

These were the original RESPs and they are still widely used today. Unfortunately, they can be extremely complicated. As with life-insurance policies, it is difficult with pooled plans to get a clear picture of the costs you will be assessed. As well, the structures of the plans can be confusing, since most of them offer at least two and sometimes more variations. Every plan is sold with a prospectus that contains all the details, but we suspect that very few people actually read them because of the density of the language in which they are written. But our advice is to try, and to ask lots of questions before making up your mind. You should also be aware that most of the companies offering pooled plans have individual plan options as well, should you prefer to go that route.

If you choose a pooled plan, your money goes into an invest-ment pool along with the contributions from all the other subscribers. Parents (or grandparents) who enrol in these plans purchase "units" on their child's behalf. The number of units purchased will ultimately determine how much money is paid out (referred to as a "scholarship"), since each unit will qualify for a designated payment. The more units that have been bought, the more money the child will receive.

Government regulations limit the type of investments these plans can make to low-risk, fixed-income securities such as guaranteed investment certificates, government and government-guaranteed bonds (federal, provincial, and municipal), Treasury bills, and NHA (National Housing Act) mortgages. As well, the pool available for scholarships may be increased by revenue earned from affinity programs (credit cards, long-distance services, etc.), life-insurance profits, and other sources.

Each year, the amount of money available in the investment pool is divided among the students who have qualified for scholarships under the plan. The terms of quali-fying vary but generally students become eligible for payments when they enter their second year at an approved post-secondary institution. The pool includes the return on the invested money plus what is known as a tontine top-up. This consists of additional funds made available to the pool because some subscribers' children do not go on to pursue higher education. It is this top-up feature that enables pooled plans to claim rates of return that may look very impressive when compared with those of mutual funds or non-pooled RESPs. The downside, of course, is that the par-ents or grandparents of the children who do not go on to benefit from scholarships lose all the interest that accumu-lated to their credit over the years (although they would get back their capital if they stayed in the plan until maturity). So one student's gain is another family's loss. The figures vary,

TONTINE TOP-UPS

Scholarships from pooled RESPs are enhanced by additional monies freed up when some beneficiaries choose not to go on to post-secondary studies. These are called tontine top-ups.

but representatives of some of the pooled programs told us that between 10 and 13 percent of the beneficiaries of matured plans do not go on to college. The percentage of plans that are discontinued before reaching maturity is quite a bit higher, and any interest earned from that money is also forfeited.

Of course, each unit purchased increases the amount of money the parents must invest. Also, sales commissions are levied on the basis of the number of units held in the plan. It's important to note that the upfront sales charges (which the plans euphemistically call membership fees or enrolment fees) are about the same for all the programs. It's easy to be fooled by this because some plans show a charge of $100 a unit while others assess at a rate of $200 a unit. On the surface, it looks like the $200 plans are double the price. However, if you check carefully, you'll find the units of the $100 plans are about half the value — so you need twice as many units to get the same end result, bringing the sales costs in line with the $200 per unit plans. Yes, it's needlessly complicated, and there seems to be no reason for this difference other than an attempt to gain a sales edge. Don't be fooled.

Typically, the parents will get back their invested capital when the plan matures, less any applicable expenses. They will be expected to use this money to pay for the first year of college expenses. Most of the plans also repay the original enrolment fees (which can run to several thousand dollars depending on the option chosen). However, you must remain in the program until maturity to get these fees back (otherwise you will probably forfeit them), and in some cases they are paid out only as part of the scholarship money,

> **MEMBERSHIP FEES**
> *All pooled plans charge "membership fees" or "enrolment fees," which are really sales commissions by another name. The amount can be substantial, so be sure you understand what you are committing to before going ahead. In most cases, these fees are repaid if you remain in the plan until maturity, but you'll forfeit them if you quit before then.*

which means the child has to qualify for such payments. (This repayment of fees may seem generous until you do some mathematical calculations. In most plans, the fees are front-end loaded, so you pay them very early in the game — they aren't spread out over the life of the program. This means the trust gets the benefit of the interest on this money over many years. For example, suppose you pay $2,000 in enrolment fees in year one. Eighteen years later, when the plan matures, you qualify to get your $2,000 back. In the meantime, however, the value of that money has grown to $7,992, assuming annual compounding at a rate of 8 percent. As you can see, the trust can well afford to refund the original fees at that point and still come out ahead, even after paying commissions to its sales representatives.)

Most pooled RESPs will provide scholarship payments for the second, third, and fourth year of university (the Children's Education Trust is somewhat different). If the student takes a three-year program and doesn't go on to postgraduate study, the money that would have been paid for the fourth-year scholarship stays in the pot and becomes part of the next tontine top-up.

There are no guarantees as to the amount each scholarship will be worth. That will depend on the interest earned by the invested money and the amount of tontine top-up available. Past results are no indication of future returns, since we are now in a period of low interest rates when investment yields are likely to be less. You'll find information on previous pay-outs in the prospectus of some of the trust funds. Take a careful look at the numbers and you'll see how the amounts dropped through the mid-nineties. For example, the Heritage Scholarship Trust Plan paid out these totals per unit as a first scholarship (that is, to students in their first year of scholarship eligibility) from 1993 to 1996:

1993	$952.76
1994	820.88
1995	750.00
1996	735.00

Part of the problem is that these plans are restricted to fixed-income investments, so they were not able to take advantage of the booming stock markets of the nineties. All the education trusts are hoping to get approval to expand their portfolios to include index-linked GICs, which would give them stock-market exposure while guaranteeing the principal. However, this had not been forthcoming from Ottawa at the time this book was prepared.

In all cases, the amount you invest will vary depending on the age of the child. The younger the child, the lower the payments required. All the programs qualify for the new Canada Education Savings Grant.

> **LOWER RETURNS**
> *Scholarships paid by pooled plans declined through the mid-nineties as yields on fixed-income securities dropped.*

In the past, these plans have typically been sold to the newborn market. However, the introduction of the CESG may change that emphasis. Ironically, the older a child is at the time of enrolment, the less the cost of the sales commission in most cases (because an older child is enrolled for fewer years).

Those are the general parameters. However, the individual pooled programs have a number of variables, so let's examine the four leading plans of this type in greater detail. The information is current as of spring 1998. Since these programs are constantly evolving, get up-to-date details before making a decision.

Heritage Scholarship Trust Fund

Investment strategy: The money in the pool is invested exclusively in government and government-guaranteed bonds. Bonds are normally not traded but are held to maturity, so returns are essentially interest only. Of the investment options open to the pooled RESPs, this approach is likely to generate the highest returns (unless active trading is used) and most of the trusts have now moved to it.

Minimum subscription: Two units.

Cost per unit: If purchased on a monthly basis, costs range from $4.85 a month for a newborn to $85.65 a month for a child age thirteen.

Enrolment fees (sales commissions): $100 per unit. Up to twenty-two units could be purchased for a newborn child, based on the government's RESP contribution limits. If the maximum number of units was purchased, the first $1,100 of contributions would go directly to commissions. So at the end of eleven months, the parents would have zero credits even though they had paid in more than a thousand dollars. After that, half of each monthly contribution goes towards commission until the full $2,200 is paid. From that point forward, all the money is credited to the account.

Administration fee: One half of one percent a year, based on the total value of capital plus accumulated interest.

Refund of capital: When the plan matures (normally in the year the child turns eighteen), all the capital, plus the membership fee, is returned to the parents. So as long as you stay in to maturity, you get your $2,200 back (using the illustration above).

Payments: Three scholarships will be paid, beginning in the second year of university. The amount of the scholarship is calculated by multiplying the number of units owned by the value assigned to each unit. In 1996, each unit was valued at $735, so a student whose family had bought twenty-two units would receive $16,170 annually for three years.

Substitutions: Currently, another person under age twenty-one can be substituted as the plan beneficiary at any time. However, the introduction of the CESG and the rules governing it will likely place a restriction of siblings only on the substitution of a new beneficiary.

Eligible educational institutions: Any that are approved by the federal government for RESP eligibility.

Plan variations: The Self-Determined Option has been specifically designed for situations in which the plan beneficiary decides to pursue two years or less of post-secondary education. The money in the plan (principal and earnings) is paid any time after the maturity date; however, the membership fees are not refundable in this case. To qualify, the plan's beneficiary (also known as the nominee) must attend a program of study of not less than three weeks at a recognized post-secondary institution within Canada, or thirteen weeks outside Canada. (The 1998 budget imposed restrictions on the amount that can be paid for short-term courses, however.)

Life-insurance protection: Optional. Coverage costs thirty-five cents per month per unit (expected to change soon) and provides life coverage as well as waiver-of-deposit protection for total disability. The coverage is up to $1,000 per unit. Provincial sales tax is extra in Quebec and Ontario.

Web site: www.home.inforamp.net/~herican (main site). Also various local sites.

For more information: 1-800-739-2101.

Canadian Scholarship Trust Plan

Investment strategy: This plan holds a larger percentage of its portfolio in NHA mortgages than the others — about 25 percent as of spring 1998. The balance is in bonds and GICs.

Minimum purchase: One-tenth of a unit.

Cost per unit: If purchased on a monthly basis, from $9.75 a month for a newborn.

Enrolment fees (sales commissions): $200 per unit in the Founder's Plan or Optional Plan (unit value is about double that of some of the other plans). Up to 23.3 units can be purchased for a newborn child under the Founder's Plan, the original program offered by this organization. For the newer Optional Plan, 22.1 units is the maximum. Commissions are spread over the first two and a half years of contributions. The one-time fee for a Millennium Plan is $50.

Refund of capital: When the plan matures, all the capital is returned to the parents, less sales commissions and ongoing depository fees. Return of capital is guaranteed.

Payments: In the Founder's Plan, three scholarships will be paid, beginning in the second year of college or university. In the Optional Plan, four scholarships will be paid, starting in the first year of an eligible post-secondary program. For the Millennium Plan, payments are at the option of the member.

Substitutions: In the Founder's Plan, a substitution for the beneficiary can be made at any time up to age twelve. After that, substitutions are limited to special circumstances, such as disability or the death of the beneficiary. In the Optional Plan, you can substitute for a beneficiary up to the maturity date of the plan. After that, substitutions are limited to family members under certain conditions. In the Millennium Plan, substitutions are allowed to age twenty-one, subject to certain conditions.

Eligible educational institutions: For the Founder's Plan, the choice is limited to traditional academic institutions. The Optional and Millennium plans provide greater choice, including technical schools, colleges, and any other institution approved by the federal government for RESPs.

Plan variations: Three. The Founder's Plan is the most rigid, limiting the right of substitution and the choice of school. If a student does not go on to qualify for the scholarships, the interest earned is forfeited and used for the benefit of other students enrolled in this program. The trade-off is that the payments will be higher (perhaps significantly so) for students in this plan because of the tontine top-up.

The Optional Plan offers greater flexibility and parents can roll any unused income earned into an RRSP or take it in cash under the rules introduced in the 1997 federal budget and amended in 1998.

The Millennium Plan is intended for families with children age thirteen and over. Unlike the other two, it is not a group program but is an individual RESP. Therefore, there is no possibility of a tontine top-up to enhance the final amount of the scholarship. The contributions are invested in the same type of fixed-income securities as the pooled money in the other plans, however. Fees in this case are a $50 one-time set-up charge and a one percent annual management fee, calculated on the value of the assets in the plan.

Life-insurance protection: Optional.

Web site: www.cst.org (main site). Also various local sites.

For more information: 1-800-387-4622.

USC (University Scholarships of Canada) Education Savings Plans

Investment strategy: Portfolio consists primarily of federal government bonds, with some provincials in the mix as well. Very little cash. As with most of the other pooled funds of this type, your core investment is essentially a bond fund. USC has an active investment committee that utilizes five investment counsellors to manage the money in the pool.

Minimum purchase: $9.80 a month (two units for a newborn).
Cost per unit: If purchased on a monthly basis, costs range from $4.90 a month for a child who is eighteen years from college to $52.50 a month for a child who is six years away.
Enrolment fees (sales commissions): $100 per unit.
Administration fee: One half of one percent a year, based on the total value of capital plus accumulated interest.
Refund of capital: When the plan matures (at a date determined by the client), all the capital is returned, net of fees.
Payments: In the Classic Plan, three scholarships will be paid beginning in the second year of post-secondary education. The same schedule applies for the Group Option of the Family Plan. In the Family Plan Self-Determined Option, payments are made as soon as the beneficiary attends a post-secondary institution.
Substitutions: In the Classic Plan, a substitution can be made for the beneficiary at any time up to the thirteenth birthday. In the Family Plan, you can substitute for a beneficiary at any time up to the maturity date of the plan.
Eligible educational institutions: Any accredited educational institution that is designated by the federal government as being eligible for RESPs.
Plan variations: Three. The Classic Plan is the least flexible, but has the highest return potential. There are two variations of the Family Plan that are more popular. The first is the Group Option, in which the student receives his or her share of the total value of the pool each year, similar to other traditional programs of this type, through the application of the tontine top-up. The student also receives an amount equal to one-third of the enrolment fee with each payment. The second is the Self-Determined Option, which allows money to be withdrawn immediately upon maturity and to be transferred to an RRSP (or taken in cash with a tax penalty) if the student does not attend college.
Life-insurance protection: Optional. Basic cost is twenty-five cents for each $10 of deposit.
Web site: www.resp-usc.com (main site). Also various local sites.
For more information: 1-800-363-7377.

The Children's Education Trust of Canada

Investment strategy: Government and government-guaranteed bonds. Unlike most of the other plans, the portfolio may be actively traded when market conditions are favourable to achieve higher rates of return.

Minimum subscription: One unit.

Cost per unit: If purchased on a monthly basis, costs range from $9.40 a month for a newborn to $119.60 a month for a child age twelve.

Enrolment fees (sales commissions): $200 per unit. If the annual-deposit method is selected, up to 23.55 units may be purchased under the Group Option. If the monthly-deposit method is chosen, up to 21.9 units may be bought. Enrolment fees are repaid as part of the scholarship payments under the Group Option. With the Self-Initiated Option, only a single enrolment fee of $200 applies; it is non-refundable.

Administration fee: One-half of one percent a year, based on the total value of capital plus accumulated interest.

Refund of capital: Returned to subscriber on the date the plan matures.

Payments: Somewhat different from the other plans, which spread the payments over three years, starting after the successful completion of year one. In this case, payments can be received over one or two years, depending on the program. A student taking a three-year B.A. would get scholarships in years two and three with a value equal to the total amount of the credits earned. A student completing a two-year diploma would get the entire pay-out in year two.

Substitutions: Up to age twenty-one.

Eligible educational institutions: Any that are approved by the federal government for RESP eligibility.

Plan variations: Two. The Group Option operates along the same general lines as the other pooled plans. The Self-Initiated Option has greater payment flexibility but does not allow for the recovery of enrolment fees or for participation in any group top-up.

Life-insurance protection: Optional. Basic coverage costs fifty cents per month per unit and provides completion insurance in the event of death or permanent disability. Also available is deposit-protection insurance, which covers job loss or temporary disability. Finally, there is child-nominee insurance, which provides term-life coverage and other types of protection for the plan beneficiary. It costs seventy-five cents per month, or $9 a year. Provincial sales tax is extra in Quebec and Ontario.

Web site: www.educationtrust.ca.

For more information: 1-800-246-1203.

Individual Plans

Individual RESPs have become more widely available in recent years. You can now get them from banks, trust companies, credit unions, mutual-fund companies, brokerage firms, some insurance companies, and financial planners. They offer much more flexibility in terms of where the savings can be invested, and they are certainly easier to understand than the pooled plans. However, each plan operates independently, so there is no tontine top-up to boost the returns for students who go on to college.

Think of an individual RESP as a personal family education-savings account for one or more children. The money can be invested in whatever way you choose, subject to the limitations of the plan you select. You can invest it conservatively in GICs and bonds, you can hold a mutual-fund portfolio, or you can even play the stock market. And there are no foreign-content limitations to worry about, which gives these plans even more investment flexibility than an RRSP.

The downside of such freedom is that the potential for serious investment losses is greater. The money in a pooled education trust is very conservatively managed. In an individual plan, it's feasible you could invest in securities that fall in value, thereby ending up with less capital than you started with. That's not a likely scenario over the long haul, but it's one that shouldn't be ignored.

You can set up a plan for one child or a family plan to cover all your kids. Most of these plans allow the maximum

NO RESTRICTIONS
Individual RESPs can invest in virtually any type of security, including mutual funds and stocks. Unlike RRSPs, there is no limit on foreign-content holdings.

flexibility possible under the law for switching beneficiaries, to reduce the chance you will forfeit your investment earnings or have to pay a penalty tax on them if a child does not go on to college.

The fees charged for these RESPs will vary, but you are unlikely to face anything like the heavy front-end load expenses charged by the pooled plans. Depending on the plan, there may be a small set-up fee (Altamira, for example, charges $40 to open an account), plus an annual trustee charge similar to that assessed on self-directed RRSPs (typically $100 to $125 a year plus GST/HST). Some plans cost even less; for instance, RBC Dominion Securities offers a regular RESP for a fee of $50 a year plus GST. And some RESPs cost nothing at all. Trimark, for example, charges no set-up fee and has waived all annual charges as well. There should be no commissions for investing in mutual funds since you would presumably buy them on a back-end-load basis (or stick entirely to no-load funds) because this is a long-term investment. If you invest in stocks in your RESP, sales commissions will apply.

NO CHARGES
Some individual RESPs can be set up with no charges of any kind. Trimark is one company to offer such a program.

Individual RESPs are fully eligible for the Canada Education Savings Grant and are governed by the same rules that apply to the pooled plans. Payments from an individual RESP, however, are more flexible than from a traditional pooled plan. They can begin as soon as the student is accepted by a qualified post-secondary institution; most pooled plans pay out nothing in the first year of college.

In most cases, contributions can be withdrawn from the plan at any time, without tax consequences.

Other Issues

There are a number of other factors that must be considered before setting up an RESP. These include:

Who should open the plan? A child may be the beneficiary of more than one RESP, as long as the total amount contributed to all of his plans does not exceed the legal maximum. But in most cases, there is usually just one plan per child (or per family, if it is a multiple plan). Assuming there is a choice, should that plan be opened by the parents or the grandparents? (Current rules don't allow them to act jointly.) In making the decision, the issues to consider are:

1. Money. Who can best carry the cost of the program?
2. Age. If the grandparents open the plan, they will likely be past the age of being able to transfer the investment earnings into an RRSP if the child does not go on to university.
3. Transferability. Only family members related by blood or adoption are eligible to be RESP beneficiaries. So if the parents own the plan, only their children can be beneficiaries if any accumulated CESG is to be protected. But if grandparents own the plan, all their children and grandchildren become eligible, providing a much greater talent pool on which to draw in the event that one or more of the beneficiaries doesn't go on to college.

Is there a lot of capital available immediately for investment? The $4,000 annual limit on RESP contributions makes these plans ineffective if the goal is to invest a significant amount of money for a child or grandchild immediately to take maximum advantage of compounding.

Should money be transferred from an in-trust account to an RESP? With the announcement of the Canada Education Savings Grant in the 1998 budget, some families who had been doing their education saving through in-trust accounts decided they would be better off switching the assets into an RESP to receive the government money. However, tax experts strongly advise against this. The reason? The money in an in-trust account belongs to the child. The capital in an RESP belongs to the contributing parent or grandparent. So moving money from an in-trust account to an RESP effectively changes the ownership. That could create some major problems with

> **TAX TRAP**
> *Don't try to transfer money from an in-trust account to an RESP to take advantage of the Canada Education Savings Grant. You could find yourself with a major tax headache if you do.*

Revenue Canada and might lead to a hefty tax reassessment.

Should it be a single-beneficiary plan or a family plan? A family plan certainly offers greater flexibility, assuming there is more than one qualified beneficiary in the family unit. However, since there is no requirement that all the beneficiaries draw equally from the program, there is some potential for inequity. For example, unless care is exercised, older children may use up most of the savings in the pot, leaving a younger child with a financial shortfall when his turn for college arrives.

◆

"So as you can see, it's not an easy decision." Henry leaned back in his chair. He had just finished giving his analysis of RESPs to the family and he was tired.

Liz shook her head in wonderment. "I'm amazed at how you've managed to digest all that," she said. "You should have been a banker."

Henry smiled. His daughter-in-law was always quick to acknowledge his contributions and he appreciated it.

"So what do you think, Dad?" Jeff asked. "Should we open one of these plans or not?"

Henry hesitated. There was really no clear-cut answer he could give them. RESPs certainly had their advantages, but there were still risks involved. "As things stand right now, I would stay away from the pooled plans," he ventured. "They're really quite expensive, and they're limited in terms of where they can invest."

"But what about an individual plan?" Liz asked. "You said they don't have to cost a lot."

"That's true," Henry admitted. "And if you had more than one child, which we hope you will, then I would say, 'Yes, open a family plan.' But right now there is just Romney. I'm sure she will grow up to be a fine scholar and want to go on to college. But the risk is always there that you could lose a lot of money if she doesn't, because of the high penalty the government would force you to pay at the end."

"So what are you saying?"

"I think the safest thing to do is to keep putting money

into an in-trust account for Romney, at least for now. If another child comes along, then you can open a family RESP that covers them both, and take advantage of these new grants in the process. There's no law that says you can't save in both ways."

Jeff looked across the table at Liz, who was holding Romney in her arms. She nodded as she prepared to feed her daughter. "Makes sense to me, Dad. Thanks."

Chapter 12

Where to Put the Money

"*I* can't believe it! I simply can't. Who would have ever thought? This little corner lot we bought thirty years ago for — how much was it, dear?" Mary still couldn't grasp all the implications of the paper she held in her hand.

"It was $32,000. I'll never forget. It seemed like a fortune at the time. We had to pay $3,000 up front, our life savings. And then I thought we'd never pay off the mortgage. It was rough."

The real-estate agent smiled. She'd heard dozens of similar stories in recent years. Immigrants who had come to Canada with little or nothing in their pockets, but who had scrimped and saved to buy commercial property in the heart of the nation's booming cities. Now those properties were in huge demand for high-rise development and were going for prices once thought to be astronomical.

Mary looked at the offer to purchase again. Her eyes fixed on the number in the centre of the page. She hadn't been mistaken. It was indeed $432,500.

Mr. Sniderman's visit of a few months back had touched off a bidding war for their piece of land. It just so happened that two developers had independently drawn up plans for transforming their block into a west-end office and retail complex. Their corner lot was the key to pulling it all together.

Once Henry became aware of this, he had sought the advice of his lawyer. The lawyer in turn had contacted both parties and arranged for bidding to be conducted on an orderly basis. The offer Mary was holding in her hands was the culmination of the process. It was firm and binding, all they had to do was sign it back.

"Thank you for bringing this around," Henry said to the agent. "I'll take it in to my lawyer's office in the morning. Unless he finds something unusual, we have a deal."

The agent brightened at the thought of a fat commission. "Don't forget, it's valid for only forty-eight hours," she cautioned. "Otherwise it will lapse."

"I know how these things work," Henry said. "Don't worry. It will get done."

After she was gone, Henry and Mary sat at the table and stared at the document.

"What does it mean for our life?" Mary said at last, breaking the silence.

"It means you won't have to work any more. It means we can live in a nice house and not over a store. It means we will have some money to invest. It means I can help the kids with Romney's education."

"Oh my," Mary exclaimed. "Such changes. How will you handle it all? Where are you going to put the money?"

◆

Deciding where to invest a lot of money is not easy. There are many factors to consider, including personal objectives, risk tolerance, age, size of family, tax situation, and debts owed. If Henry is smart (and we know he is), he will find a financial adviser whom he trusts and respects to help him manage the money once the deal on the property closes.

But we can offer him some advice about how to invest the portion he plans to put aside for baby Romney. You'll recall that he set up a small in-trust account for her a while ago, into which he paid an initial $100 to invest in a mutual fund. That account can now be used as the vehicle for investing a much larger sum of money on Romney's behalf.

After going over all the finances carefully, Henry and Mary

will decide how much to put into the in-trust account as a one-time capital contribution. The account has been structured with Mary as the contributor and Henry as the trustee. Now how should the money be invested?

As we've already learned, the income-attribution rules come into play in this situation. So Henry wants to keep any interest or dividend income to an absolute minimum. The focus needs to be on capital gains, which will devolve to Romney for tax purposes.

However, capital gains imply risk since they are usually (although not always) the result of stock trades, either directly or indirectly through equity mutual funds. Henry and Mary don't want to take a lot of risk with the money, so one of the key objectives is to find securities that will minimize the chance of loss while generating above-average capital gains over the years.

Because the money is going into an in-trust account, there are no geographic limits on where it can be invested. The 20 percent foreign-content rule that bedevils RRSP investors does not come into play here. So the investments may be made anywhere in the world.

NO LIMITS
There are no geographic limits on how the money in an in-trust account or an RESP can be invested. The 20 percent foreign-content rule that governs RRSPs and pension plans does not apply.

Of course, it's not a good idea to put all the eggs in one basket. A single investment, even in a top-grade mutual fund, can conceivably go sour. The goal should be to create a well-diversified portfolio, one that can be held for several years with minimum changes.

The easiest way to achieve this is with mutual funds. Each fund invests in a broad portfolio of securities, thereby limiting investor risk by spreading the money across a range of company stocks. In the situation we are looking at here, the best strategy would be to set up a portfolio of, say, five top-quality funds for Romney, each of which brings a different dimension to the total package.

Of course, we are looking for funds that have excellent track records and good management. But there's something else to consider. In this case, funds that historically pay out high distributions are not desirable, especially if any portion of the distribution is dividends or interest, which are taxable in the hands of the contributor. The best mutual funds for this type of portfolio pay no distributions (which means there is not a lot of trading in the portfolio). Or, if distributions are paid, they are almost exclusively in the form of capital gains.

Unfortunately, some excellent mutual funds will not be available to Henry and Mary because the initial minimum contribution requirements are higher than the amount of money they will have to invest for Romney. Fine companies such as Bissett & Associates, ABC Funds, Phillips, Hager & North, GBC, and Sceptre are likely to be out of their price range. However, there is still a broad range of choices available.

AVOID DISTRIBUTIONS
Mutual funds that pay high annual distributions are not good candidates for an in-trust investment account, especially if the distributions include considerable amounts of interest or dividends.

Here are five funds that would fit very nicely into Romney's in-trust education account. There are many others, but these give you an idea of what to look for.

Templeton Growth Fund

The Templeton organization is now based in Fort Lauderdale, Florida, but it actually got its start in Canada back in the mid-fifties with this now-legendary fund. The company's style is one of value investing, and its analysts scour the globe for stocks that meet their rigid criteria. Essentially, they are looking for securities that are cheap at their current price, because the country is out of favour, because the particular industry is going through a bad patch, or simply because the market hasn't yet recognized the inherent value of the stock. Although it is impossible to invest in the stock market without risk, this approach is considered to be the most conservative among the various mutual-fund management styles.

KEEP THE RISK LOW
Look for mutual funds that employ a conservative stock selection style. Templeton Growth Fund is a good example.

Templeton Growth Fund invests throughout the world, without limitation. It has been a sound, solid performer for many, many years. It is never at the top end of the scale, but the returns are almost always better than average for the industry. Over the ten-year period to May 31, 1998, the fund generated an average annual return of almost 15 percent, which is outstanding.

The dividend pay-out record fits our profile well. In 1998, investors received a total of $1.30 a unit, all of which was realized capital gains.

AIC Value Fund

Many readers will be familiar with the name of Warren Buffett. He is one of the world's most successful investors, and is known as the Oracle of Omaha, which is where he resides. His investment company, Berkshire Hathaway, has become a legend and is the most expensive stock traded on the New York Stock Exchange.

Buffett's style is deceptively simple. He identifies top companies in expanding business areas and holds the stocks forever. Some of his favourites over the years have been McDonald's, Gillette, Coca-Cola, and American Express.

Most people couldn't afford to buy even a single share of Berkshire Hathaway (they were trading for more than C$100,000 each in the spring of 1998). But anyone with $500 in their pocket can purchase the Buffett style by investing in the Hamilton, Ontario–based AIC Value Fund. This fund emulates the Buffett approach by investing in shares of the companies he likes, as well as holding stock in Berkshire Hathaway. It has been very successful since its creation in 1990, with a five-year average annual compound rate of return of 28.3 percent to May 31, 1998.

BUYING BUFFETT
Shares in investment guru Warren Buffett's Berkshire Hathaway company were selling for more than $100,000 each in the spring of 1998. But you can buy into his highly successful investment style for just $500 through a Hamilton, Ontario, mutual fund.

Since Buffett is a buy-and-hold investor, this is a buy-and-hold fund. That means distributions are almost non-existent.

In 1997, for example, no pay-outs were made to unitholders. In some situations, that can create a tax problem down the road, when units are sold and gains crystallized. But in this particular case, the no-distribution approach works very effectively in meeting our goals for the education portfolio.

Ivy Canadian Fund

Although the Canadian stock market has not been as strong in recent years as those of the U.S. and Europe, our country has excellent economic prospects. With the federal deficit eliminated and the political situation in Quebec apparently off the boil, at least for the time being, the outlook for Canadian equities is good.

So there should be at least one Canadian stock fund in Romney's education portfolio. We have selected Mackenzie Financial's Ivy Canadian Fund because of its conservative style, good track record, and limited distributions.

Ivy Canadian is managed by Jerry Javasky, a seasoned veteran who uses a value approach to select his stocks. He limits risk in his portfolio through his choice of securities and by holding large cash balances in turbulent markets. As a result, since its creation in 1992 the fund has established a reputation of being among the safest of its type. That doesn't guarantee it will never lose money, but so far it has recorded a profit in every calendar year of its existence. Average annual compound rate of return for the five years to May 31, 1998, was 15.6 percent.

> **CANADA'S PROSPECTS GOOD**
>
> *Although Canadian stock markets haven't kept pace with those of the U.S. and Europe in recent years, our future prospects look bright thanks to a much-improved financial situation in Ottawa and reduced pressure from the Quebec separatists.*

Since Javasky doesn't do a lot of trading, distributions are kept to a minimum. There were none at all in 1997.

AGF American Growth Class

No investment portfolio of this type would be complete without a fund that specializes in the big names of corporate America. That's what we find here: General Electric, Microsoft,

Intel, Home Depot, Lockheed — the bluest of the blue chips. The fund has been managed since 1993 by Steven Rogers and he has done an outstanding job with it, using what is known as a bottom-up stock selection approach (which means he focuses on corporate fundamentals such as profits, revenues, and debt levels). The safety record of this fund is one of the best in the U.S. equity category, which further enhances its appeal for Romney's portfolio.

Average annual compound rate of return over the five years to May 31, 1998, was an excellent 24.4 percent. There were no distributions in 1997.

Fidelity International Portfolio Fund

The Boston-based Fidelity organization offers some top-performing international funds to Canadian investors. This one has a diversified portfolio that incorporates their best picks from around the world. The fund has been run by Fidelity senior vice-president Dick Habermann since 1993 and searches out stocks with above-average growth potential. The companies in the mix tend to be of the blue-chip variety, such as pharmaceutical giant Merck & Company, Safeway food stores, AT&T, and Ford Motor Company. Although recent emphasis has been on U.S. stocks, the portfolio is spread around the world.

Results have been very good. Fidelity's five-year average annual compound rate of return to May 31, 1998 (approximately covering the period since Habermann took over), was 17.8 percent.

The one negative with this fund is its relatively high distribution pattern, a result of active trading in the portfolio. In 1997, for example, the fund paid out ninety-seven cents a unit to its shareholders. However, most of that (just over ninety-five cents a unit) came as capital gains. Only about a cent and a half per unit was dividend income, which would be attributed back to the contributor for tax purposes.

So, to summarize, here is the sample investment portfolio we recommend for an education in-trust account:

Templeton Growth Fund	20%
AIC Value Fund	20%
Ivy Canadian Fund	20%
AGF American Growth Class	20%
Fidelity International Portfolio Fund	20%

Any financial adviser or discount brokerage firm can easily build such a fund portfolio for you. All the funds should be purchased initially on a back-end-load basis (you pay no commission when you buy), since these are intended as long-term holds.

AVOID COMMISSIONS
Buy your funds on a back-end-load basis to avoid having to pay sales charges.

An investment in an in-trust account must be monitored carefully. The performance should be reviewed regularly and capital gains should be crystallized periodically along the way to avoid a huge tax bill when the child is ready to start drawing on the assets of the plan for college expenses. This can be done simply by switching some assets from one fund to another in the same group for a period of time. As far as Revenue Canada is concerned, a switch is the same as a sell.

For example, let's suppose that the original amount invested was $5,000. Five years pass and the portfolio grows by an average of 15 percent annually over that time. That means it would now be worth slightly more than $10,000, so the beneficiary would be sitting on a capital gain of $5,000 and change. At this point, the trustee could instruct the financial adviser to do some switching. They might move the Templeton Growth Fund assets into Templeton International Stock Fund, the AIC Value Fund holdings into AIC Advantage Fund, etc. Keeping the money within the same fund family eliminates any back-end load charges.

These moves would leave the child beneficiary with capital gains of a little more than $5,000. A tax return would be filed on his or her behalf, declaring this amount. No taxes would be payable, however, because the child's entitlement to the personal tax credit would effectively shelter the profits. Once the gains have been claimed, the clock is reset and new capital gains are calculated from the price paid for

CRYSTALLIZE GAINS

Take capital gains in the in-trust portfolio from time to time to avoid having to pay substantial taxes later. This can be done by switching assets from one fund to another within the same family. The profits can be sheltered using the child's personal tax credit.

the holdings in the new funds. If desired, the money can be switched back to the original funds a few months later. The larger the amount of money invested on a child's behalf, the more often it will probably be necessary to crystallize and declare some capital gains.

As we learned earlier, when the child turns eighteen, the assets that are held in the in-trust account at that time become his or her property as far as Revenue Canada is concerned. Since the child is now of legal age, the income-attribution rules no longer apply.

At this point, a switch in investment strategy is recommended. We are now getting close to the time when the child-turned-adult will be ready to begin college. Retaining the investment assets in equity mutual funds is no longer advisable in such circumstances. At this stage, the goal should be to minimize the chance of any sudden losses due to a stock-market correction, while at the same time having the assets in liquid form so they can be drawn out easily.

So the emphasis of the portfolio should shift from equity funds to low-risk fixed-income and money funds. The composition of such a portfolio might look like this:

Money-market funds	20%
Mortgage funds	15%
Short-term bond funds	20%
Regular bond funds	20%
Equity funds	25%

We retain about a quarter of the portfolio in equity funds for continued growth potential, but this will gradually decline as the student progresses through university. By the time she is ready to begin her final year, there should be no assets left in equity funds and the bulk of the cash should be in money-market funds, short-term deposits, or bank accounts.

The beauty of this strategy is that it minimizes taxes for both the parents or the grandparents and the student. Very little income will be attributed to the contributor for tax purposes. In the meantime, the student, because of the periodic recognition of capital gains, will be left with what amounts to a tax-paid account worth many thousands of dollars (at 15 percent annual growth, $5,000 will be worth more than $60,000

> **CHANGING STRATEGIES**
> *As the child approaches university age, the money should be shifted out of equity funds and into lower-risk securities like bond funds and money-market funds.*

after eighteen years). This is a different scenario from an RESP, where all the income earned is taxable in the student's hands when it is withdrawn. Depending on how much money is withdrawn and the tax credits available, that could lead to a tax bill of several thousand dollars a year.

The investing strategy for a self-directed RESP would be somewhat different. In this case, you don't need to be concerned about focusing exclusively on capital gains, or on distribution policies if mutual funds are used. Here again, foreign content is unlimited, so that does not have to be a concern.

Because an RESP portfolio will be built gradually over time, we suggest starting with a good balanced mutual fund. This will provide immediate diversification over a range of securities (stocks, bonds, Treasury bills) and will reduce risk.

> **RESP INVESTING**
> *More diversification can be built into a self-directed RESP because the income-attribution rules do not apply. A good balanced fund is a recommended starting-point.*

There are many good balanced funds that would fit the bill. Here are a couple of good choices:

Ivy Growth and Income Fund

This fund is managed by Jerry Javasky, the same person who runs Ivy Canadian, which we recommended for an in-trust portfolio, so many of the same stocks will be held in this fund as well. The difference is that this fund will also hold some of its assets in bonds — the mix will vary depending on market conditions and the economic outlook. The results here haven't been quite as good as those of Ivy Canadian. The five-year average annual compound rate of return to May 31, 1998, was 14.4 percent, more than one percent below that of its stablemate. But the risk factor is somewhat lower here.

AGF American Tactical Asset Allocation Fund

Since you don't have to worry about foreign-content restrictions, you could start off the RESP by investing exclusively in the world's strongest economy, the United States. This fund uses a computer model to distribute assets among stocks, bonds, and cash, depending on the outlook. It has been highly successful, with a five-year average annual compound rate of return of 14.9 percent to May 31, 1998.

As money builds in the RESP, more diversification becomes possible. Any of the stock funds already mentioned could be added to the mix (although it would not make a lot of sense to hold both Ivy Growth and Income and Ivy Canadian, since you'd be buying pretty much the same thing). A first-rate bond fund, such as Altamira Bond, could also be added. The portfolio of a mature self-directed RESP might look like this:

Altamira Bond Fund	20%
AGF American Tactical Asset Allocation Fund	20%
Templeton Growth Fund	20%
AIC Value Fund	20%
Ivy Canadian Fund	20%

Here again, as the youngster comes within a couple of years of being ready for college, it's a good idea to reduce risk and make the portfolio more liquid so the money can be readily drawn upon as needed.

Universal Life Insurance

An alternative to the in-trust account and the RESP that some parents have chosen is universal life insurance. In some ways, this is an apples and oranges comparison, since part of the money in this case is spent on life-insurance coverage for the child.

"If the objective is strictly to accumulate cash, universal

life doesn't compete with an RESP, especially now with the new government grants," acknowledges Art Poulton, a senior sales executive with Regina-based Crown Life. "But if parents want to do some longer-term financial planning that includes an education-savings component, this option is worth careful consideration."

It works like this. In a universal life policy, part of the premium is used to pay for the insurance coverage and the balance goes into an accumulating fund, which is invested in a tax-sheltered environment. The investment options will vary from one company to another but are normally quite conservative (Crown Life offers a selection of index-linked accounts). There are no foreign-content limits to be concerned with.

Let's assume a parent takes out a universal life policy for a newborn child instead of going the in-trust account or RESP route. The parent becomes the legal owner of the plan; the child is the insured. The amount of the annual premium is variable. We asked Poulton to run some examples on his computer using Crown Life rates; the numbers may differ for other insurance companies but should be in the same ballpark.

Using a child under age one and assuming $300,000 in life-insurance coverage, the annual premium ranged from a minimum of $771 a year to a maximum of $2,724. Choosing the minimum premium and staying with it throughout would not produce an adequate education fund; at the end of twenty years, the plan would have a cash value of only $19,555, assuming an average annual compound rate of return of 8 percent.

But if the parent topped up the premium to the maximum allowable by law (Revenue Canada has some complex rules that govern this), the picture changes dramatically. After twenty years, the cash value of the policy is $114,396, most of which can be withdrawn for education (or any other) purpose. That should be more than enough to pay the college bills for four years.

As with an RESP, when money is withdrawn from the policy, it is taxed at the insured's marginal rate (assuming the policy has been transferred to him or her by the parent). If the offspring is now a student, any tax payable should be very low.

One advantage of universal life over an in-trust account is that there is no age at which control of the plan's assets must automatically be transferred from parent to child. That decision is strictly in the parent's hands. So if the eighteen-year-old turns out to be a rebellious ingrate who has no intention of going to college, the parent can retain control of the invested money indefinitely in hopes time will mellow the child or at least instil some degree of responsibility (however, when the parent dies, all the assets in the plan pass to the insured).

Universal life also has an advantage over an RESP in that there is no financial penalty if the child does not go on to university. The money remains in the plan and can be used for any other purpose.

Plus, the life-insurance coverage remains in place long after the student has graduated and has joined the working world, providing cheap ongoing protection for his or her family.

The downside of this approach is that you pay a good chunk of money for life-insurance coverage for a young child, which, to our mind, is a questionable expense. Does a child with no dependents really need life insurance? A life-insurance salesperson would, of course, answer "yes" because it guarantees future life insurability at low rates. But we would suggest that the money would be better used for the children's immediate needs and/or invested on their behalf.

However, that trade-off may be acceptable if some of the other features of this type of education savings are important to you, or if you want to put a lifetime insurance policy into place for your child at the cheapest possible rate.

◆

"Well, it's finished," Henry said with satisfaction. "We've done what we can for Romney. Now let's hope everything works out as we've planned."

"Well, that's good. But now could you spend some time thinking about us? Like where we are going to live? And what we're going to work at?" That was Mary, always practical.

The deal was done. The money was deposited, the store was gone, soon to be bulldozed in the name of progress. They were staying temporarily in a furnished apartment because the developer had insisted on a fast closing as a *quid pro quo* for what he said was the outrageous price he was paying. So Henry and Mary had to pack their belongings in a hurry and put them into storage while they decided where they would buy a house. Somewhere close to Jeff and Liz, that was certain. They'd already seen a couple of attractive little houses just a few streets away.

But what would he work at? He'd hardly had time to think about it, with all the excitement of the sale. He knew one thing, however. After thirty years, he was happy the store was gone. The hours were long, and in the past few years he had become increasingly worried about Mary being in the shop, with all the hold-ups and all. Whatever the future held, he knew it would bring better times.

Chapter 13

Summing Up

We hope that Henry Quan's persistence has succeeded in making you much more knowledgeable about the whole issue of education savings and preparing a child for university. But we realize there has been a lot to absorb in these pages. So this chapter is designed to bring our key points together in a single place, for easy reference. If you want to refresh yourself about the details, we've included the relevant chapter references in each case.

The Loan Trap

Tuition fees have been going up at a much faster pace than the rate of inflation, and that is likely to accelerate as governments cut back on the money available to colleges and universities. As a result, many students are trying to make it through school with loans, and then discovering they can't repay them. The rate of student-loan bankruptcies is increasing at an alarming pace, and the average amount owed has risen from $17,000 in 1995 to $25,000 in 1998. Clearly, this is not the solution to the problem. (Chapter Two)

Get Started

We're full of good intentions. The problem is we're not doing anything about them. A recent poll found that 77 percent of parents with children under eight intend to start an education savings plan. But only 24 percent of parents with children at university actually did it. There's a big slippage along the way, and that may result in hundreds of thousands of young people missing out on higher education in the years to come. Moral: If you think it's a good idea, get going now. (Chapter Four)

Groom Your Child for a Scholarship

Millions of dollars are available every year through scholarships in Canada, some of which almost always goes begging. Some of the awards are worth tens of thousands of dollars over a three- or four-year academic program, so they are certainly worth pursuing. Scholarship committees want to see community involvement. Good marks are important, but without a strong record of participation in volunteer activities, a student has little chance of winning a top award. Parents should encourage their youngsters from an early age to participate in organizations they enjoy and to assume leadership positions when they are ready. This does not mean pushing them into activities they don't like. Rather, create the opportunity and let them make their own choices. Part-time work that may interfere with volunteer activities should be kept within strict limits. As they approach college age, students should apply for every scholarship for which they are eligible. (Chapter Five)

Be Careful of the Income-Attribution Rules

Parents and grandparents who put money aside for a child's future education face a tax barrier known as the income-attribution rule. Basically, it states that any interest or dividends earned on money invested in a child's name reverts to the contributing parent or grandparent for tax purposes. But you can get around the problem by investing for capital gains, since these are deemed to belong to the child for tax purposes. (Chapter Six)

Child Tax Benefit Payments

Although they are taxed in the parents' hands, payments received from the Child Tax Benefit may be invested in the youngster's name without worrying about the attribution rules. This had also previously been the case with Family Allowance payments; when that program was replaced by the Child Tax Benefit, this rule was maintained. Cheques should be deposited directly to an in-trust account set up for the child, and that account should be kept pure for tax purposes — don't put any other monies into it. All income earned by this account, from whatever source, will belong to the child for tax purposes. (Chapter Seven)

Non-Attributable Money

Besides Child Tax Benefit payments, children can receive income from a few other sources that will not be subject to the attribution rules when invested. These include employment earnings (part-time jobs), inheritances, gifts from non-relatives, and gifts from relatives who live outside the country and therefore do not come under Revenue Canada's jurisdiction. (Chapter Eight)

In-Trust Accounts

Setting up an in-trust account for a child is easy to do. However, most of the in-trust accounts in Canada are improperly structured and leave the parents open to potential problems with Revenue Canada in the future. To meet the government's requirements, an in-trust account needs three participants: a beneficiary (the child), a contributor, and a trustee. The contributor and the trustee must not be the same person; however, Revenue Canada says that a husband and a wife may fill the two roles. Parents and grandparents should be aware that the money in an in-trust account is the legal property of the child. When the beneficiary reaches the age of majority, he or she can do anything with the money — regardless of the contributor's original intentions in setting up the account. So there is a risk the money in an account meant for education savings could be spent on high living by a profligate child. (Chapter Nine)

Formal Trusts

You can get around many of the problems of in-trust accounts by setting up a formal trust with instructions that the proceeds be applied for education purposes. However, this is an expensive alternative and is really an option for only the well-to-do. (Chapter Nine)

Government Education Grants

The 1998 federal budget announced a new initiative in government support for education savings, the Canada Education Savings Grant (CESG). These grants are paid into an RESP at a rate of 20 percent of the contribution, to a maximum of $400 a year. A newborn baby whose parents opened an RESP immediately could receive up to $7,200 under the program over eighteen years. If the money compounded at a rate of 8 percent annually, the CESGs would add about $15,000 to the money available for college. (Chapter Ten)

RESP Dangers

Registered education savings plans offer a way of building investment savings in a tax-sheltered environment. However, there is a risk involved. If the child does not go on to college and no substitute beneficiary is available (such as a brother or sister), the CESG money that has accumulated in the plan reverts to the government, along with the investment income it has earned. Other investment income can be transferred into the RRSP of the plan contributor, but only if there is adequate contribution room available (in some cases, that could be tens of thousands of dollars). Otherwise, the income can be withdrawn from the plan, but only on payment of a surtax, which amounts to an additional 20 percent on top of the applicable marginal rate. (Chapter Ten)

Pooled versus Individual RESPs

For many years, pooled RESPs dominated the field. However, they are saddled with high front-end load charges (although the fees are usually refunded at maturity) and the managers are limited in the type of investments they can use. In recent years, individual RESPs have become more popular. The cost is lower (some of the plans are even free) and the range of allowable securities is much greater. (Chapter Eleven)

In-Trust Investment Strategies (Early)

There are no foreign-content limits on investments in an RESP or an in-trust account. This allows for much greater flexibility than is available to RRSP investors. For an in-trust account, we recommend that the focus be placed on equity mutual funds that pay little or no distributions. This ensures that most of the investment earnings will be in the form of capital gains, which are taxable in the child's hands. The trustee of the plan should crystallize some gains from time to time to ensure that there won't be a big tax bite when the child is ready for college. RESP accounts can be more flexible in their fund selection. (Chapter Twelve)

In-Trust Investment Strategies (Late)

When a child who is the beneficiary of an in-trust account comes of age, the investment emphasis should change from capital gains to more conservative interest-bearing securities. The reason? At this stage, with college just a year or two away, it is important to protect the accumulated capital against sudden loss and to have the money readily available for withdrawal as required. (Chapter Twelve)

RESP Investment Strategies

RESP investors don't need to focus exclusively on capital gains, so the plans can be more diversified, thus reducing risk. A good starting-point is a balanced fund, such as Ivy Growth and Income or AGF American Tactical Asset Allocation. As the plan matures, other types of investments may be added, including bond funds and equity funds. As the child approaches college age, steps should be taken to reduce the risk in the portfolio and to have the assets in a form that can be easily drawn on as needed. (Chapter Twelve)

Universal Life Plans

Universal life insurance can be used as an alternative to RESPs and in-trust accounts. There are a couple of advantages to doing this. First, there is no set age at which the assets automatically pass from the parent to the child, which is one of the concerns with an in-trust account. Second, if the child does not go on to higher education, the money can be used for any other purpose with no penalty. However, you will not build as large an education fund in this way as with an RESP or an in-trust account because some of your payments will cover the cost of life insurance on the child. (Chapter Twelve)

Chapter 14

June 2020:
A Woman's Place Is . . . in University

"*R*avi! You look so smart, I didn't recognize you." Romney had spotted her friend as he came through the stone archway beside New College, heading for the waving flags and the sound of the band.

"It feels really weird," said Ravi, tugging at the collar of his blue shirt. "Like I never wore a suit before."

"Ravi, you know my parents, and these are my grandparents, Mary and Henry. Grandma, Grampa, this is Ravi Chowdhury. He was in my course."

Handshakes, smiles. "I'm sure glad Romney *was* in my course," said Ravi, "or I don't think I'd be here graduating today."

"Aw, come on, Ravi. You're the smart one. He's headed for big things, Dad. He already has two job offers, one from Microsoft Canada."

"Congratulations," said Jeff.

"I'm serious, Mr. Quan. Without Romney, I would have been in a fix. School has been such a hassle. There was never time for anything. A lot of times I had to depend on her notes."

"Ravi was holding down two jobs all the way through," explained Romney.

"Some jobs!" said Ravi. "Evenings at the sub shop, then

working on the phones telemarketing — everything from trips to Florida to phoney contests. They don't exactly look great on my résumé."

"Why did you have to work so hard?" inquired Henry. "Wasn't school work more important?"

"Sure was. But I needed the cash. My parents — there they are over there, I'll bring them over in a minute to meet you — well, I was eight when we came here from India. My dad, he works in security at the airport even though he's got a degree, and my mom, well, all she could get was a factory job. So there was not much money. And there's my brother and sister to think about, too."

"Were you able to get loans?" asked Liz.

"I got some, but my dad wasn't too keen on it. It's our tradition, I guess. You don't go into debt if you can help it. That's why I worked."

The band had struck up "The Maple Leaf Forever," Canada's stirring unofficial anthem, which, with its modernized words, had become a fixture at all public events. The upbeat tempo was the signal for the scattered crowd of graduates and their parents to make briskly for the seats in front of the platform.

"We'd better get going," said Jeff. "Ravi, we'll come over and say hi to your parents after."

◆

The gowns took Mary by surprise. She had never been to a graduation ceremony before, and she expected everyone to be in their business greys and blues. Instead, as the university officials and professors took their seats on the platform, it was like the flowerbed in her backyard coming into bloom. They wore gowns ranging in colour from the lightest pink to the deepest scarlet, from satiny white and daffodil yellow to monkshood purple, each representing the university from which they had graduated. If someone had told her it would all look so — well, pretty — she never would have believed them. She took a shy sideways glance at her granddaughter. Romney's face was shining. Mary was glad that the girl was as excited as she was by the whole affair.

Excited yes, but Romney could not possibly have comprehended the whirl of impressions going through her grandmother's mind. Mary remembered herself as a girl in Hong Kong, tending the chickens in the long dark shed behind her parents' house. She remembered, at eighteen, taking the long flight to some place named Canada where, they told her, everyone was rich and happy.

However, they had neglected to mention the hard work. When she and Henry were married, they thought their fortunes were made when they were able to buy the little variety store downtown. But again, no one told her about the long hours, about staying open from six in the morning until eleven at night when there was nothing to do except climb into bed and go to sleep quickly before the alarm went off again.

What was the point of it all — the years of drudgery, of scrimping? Yes, she could see now — this was the point of it all. This sea of excited faces, of proud parents and grandparents, and herself among them. She could never have known it, but all those struggles were directed towards this one point, this one day.

There had been other days. The time Jeff brought home that beautiful girl with the golden hair to their little apartment above the store, and she and Henry had felt abashed in front of her. They had wondered whether Jeff was doing the right thing, but then it all turned out so well and Liz became the daughter to her that she had never had.

There was the day she had first held Romney, a little red and wrinkled creature, in her arms, and later, when she had first held Julian. There had been the Sunday afternoons when, with the store closed for a few hours, they had all gone to the public gardens to sit on the grass, just like other families, drinking tea from flasks, talking and watching the grandchildren run here and there.

"Romney Anderson-Quan!" Mary jumped as her granddaughter's name was announced. She had been so lost in her reverie, she had only heard the speeches, the choir singing, as if from far away.

She watched as Romney, one of the first to be called because of the *A* in her name, made her way to the platform, her father darting behind, his video camera trained on her. Mary was pleased to see that nice friend of Romney's, the boy from India, had been called up, too. Now the two of them were kneeling on a funny little bench before that very important looking lady, while behind them two of the professors placed brilliant yellow hoods around their shoulders.

Now Romney and the boy were getting up. They turned, and Romney smiled and waved towards where they were sitting. Mary felt a nudge at her arm. Henry wordlessly handed her the white handkerchief she had earlier folded and put in his top pocket. She had not realized she was crying.

◆

"Solar cars in Vancouver! Just about every time I was there to see my brother it was raining or else cloudy," said Henry, his voice almost drowned out by the persistent chirping song of a cardinal in the honey locust tree at the bottom of the garden. The family was eating lunch on the terrace, the midday sun filtering through the purple wisteria overhead.

"Not just solar, Grampa," explained Romney. "They're combined with a hydrogen fuel cell so you never get stranded."

"Did I ever tell you about the Chevy Camaro I had when I met your grandma? It was red and could it go!"

"I know, Dad, you've told us about it often enough," said Jeff, serving the papaya and brown rice. "It used to run on gasoline, and I bet it used about a hundred times as much fuel as the cars Romney will be working on at Ballard."

With her honours degree in engineering, Romney had been given her choice of several jobs, including an intriguing offer from the NASA Mars space-station program. But she'd opted for terra firma and an exciting job helping develop the new line of solar-powered Beetle cars for Volkswagen, a co-op project at the vast Ballard complex in British Columbia.

"Take your umbrella, that's all I'm saying," said Henry.

"Oh, Dad, you're just grumpy because you won't be seeing your favourite granddaughter so often," said Liz. "Darling, I must admit I'm just a bit envious. Everything has gone so right for you. And if you ever change your mind, now that you've got your degree, you can switch and do whatever you like."

"That's how it is these days," said Henry. "Chop and change. People are never satisfied."

"You can talk," Liz taunted him. "Look at yourself: One day running a store, then writing a newsletter, now a crossing guard. What next?"

"Lucky they never asked for my degree," chuckled Henry.

"I don't know about your degree, Grampa," Romney chided him, "but you've been keeping something from me. Dad says it was you and Mom who were responsible for me going to university. But nobody's ever told me what exactly happened."

"Oh, that was nothing, nothing at all," said her grandfather. "Eh, Liz?"

"I'm not in on any secret conspiracy with you, Dad," said his daughter-in-law, laughing. "You better tell or I will."

Henry grinned. "Okay, I'll come clean. Jeff, give me another cup of coffee will you?"

"Well?" said Romney.

"January 28, 1998 — that's the day you were born, right?"

"You know it is."

"Right, I will never forget. And your grandmother won't forget it either. Such a fool she made of herself. Rushing me down to the department store and into the baby section. A pink dress, she had to have a pink dress. For her first granddaughter. They had millions of pink dresses down there. She must have been looking for an hour before she found the right one. That was probably the last time you ever wore pink. Blue I always saw you in after."

"Get on with the story, old man," said Mary, kicking his foot under the table.

"Okay, okay. Don't rush me. It's not easy remembering everything. Right about that time I started reading in the newspapers about kids at university getting into big trouble because of student loans. Not only that, they were saying that down the road, you'd need a heck of a lot more money if you wanted to go to university."

Henry pointed an accusing finger at his wife. "Not pink dresses this girl needs! Remember, I told you that? Someday she needs to go to university. She needs money. And you told me not to be foolish, right?" Mary nodded reluctantly.

Henry did not let up: "We're not rich people who can pay for our grandchildren to go to university. That's what you said, remember? Well, you were right. We did not have a lot of money. But brains we have. I thought a lot about it. I made a few phone calls. There was that guy I met at the park. And — remember, Liz — you took me along to meet that friend of yours who worked in the big mutual-fund office? And what I found out was a big shock. They told me four years at university, by the time you were ready, would cost maybe $80,000. Ha, ha, it turned out to be a lot more than that.

"Then, I guess it would have been May and we went to the park one Sunday. It was so much fun with you and Jeff and little Romney." His daughter-in-law nodded and put her hand on his arm. Romney noticed her mother's eyes were moist.

"I remember," Liz said at last. "The others had gone for a walk down by the lake and you told me we had to be thinking about Romney's university education — right away. I didn't understand the need for the big rush. I mean, Jeff and I didn't have much money to put away, and I didn't think you did either."

He looked fondly at her. "But I told you," he said, a note of triumph in his voice, "that we don't have to be rich in dollars. We only have to be rich in time."

"What do you mean, Grampa?"

"Even a little bit of money, if you have enough time, grows into a big — what do you call it? — nest egg," said the old man. "So we just had to get started."

"My job was to work on your father," said Liz. "And Grampa was going to make more inquiries."

"And, boy, did your mother work on me!" said Jeff, laughing. "I was just setting up in business at the time, and there was no money to spare. But your mother and grandfather more or less strong-armed me along to see a financial adviser, and she showed us how it could all be done. And to cut a very long story short, the result, my dear, was that, when the time came, both you and Julian were able to go to university without worrying about debt. And now there's still enough money in the fund if either of you ever decides you want to pursue your master's."

"Jeff," said his wife, "don't forget the contribution your parents made."

"Aw, forget it," said Henry. "We were selling the business, and as your grandmother said, we didn't need all that money. So we put a lump sum into your education fund. If I told you how much it was, you'd laugh, but like I said, it's time that works wonders."

"I don't know what to say," said Romney. "I feel kind of embarrassed. I always knew there was a university fund for Julian and me. I guess for that reason we always thought we would be going to university. But I never really thought how the money came to be there."

Romney reached out and grasped first her grandparents' and then her parents' hands. "Thank you, all of you. I never realized how much you had been thinking about the future, even when Julian and I were still in diapers. I love you."

"Hey, wait a minute," said her father. "You're not the only one with something to celebrate. See what I have here!" From under the food trolley, where he had obviously placed it ready for his announcement, Jeff produced a fat university course calendar. "Next September, I'm starting music studies. It might take me a few years to get my degree, but I don't aim to be left behind by everyone else in the family."

"I don't know if we can afford it, Dad," laughed Romney. "We'd better go and see the financial adviser."

Appendix 1

Know the Tax Rules

Tax breaks for students and their families are nowhere near as generous as some Canadians feel they should be, especially given the rapidly escalating costs of higher education. As one frustrated parent wrote to one of the authors:

"Why is it that parents with adult university students living at home have so few tax breaks? We feed them, pay their tuition and everything else, and yet we can't claim anything for it unless they transfer unused tuition credits to us.

"If I take a client out to lunch, I can write off half the cost. But for a child in college, nothing. It's obvious the tax laws were not written with the average person in mind.

"I believe investing in my children should be totally tax-deductible, regardless of their age. At the very least, the age limit for dependent children should be raised to twenty-one, or higher for those who have chosen to go to college or university rather than to go to jail."

Strong words. However, the government does not appear to share this view. Instead of easing the financial pressure on all parents through tax advantages, they have instead opted for programs such as the Millennium Fund, which will benefit only a relatively small percentage of Canadian students and their families.

Perhaps that will change in the future. But in the meantime, it's important to understand the tax advantages that are available so you can take advantage of them if you're eligible. Here's a run-down of the most important ones.

Tuition Tax Credit

Tuition fees have always been eligible for this tax credit. Now, you are also allowed to claim other college or university fees such as athletic and health-service assessments. But some charges, such as student-association fees, are not eligible. The fees must relate to courses you took during the year for which the credit is being claimed, and must total more than $100. If you are attending a university outside the country, the tuition costs may also be claimed, provided you were enrolled full-time in a degree course for a period of at least thirteen consecutive weeks. In all cases, special forms must be completed to make the claim; consult the General Income Tax Guide for full details.

Books, Residence Fees, Etc.

No tax relief is available for the cost of books, equipment, computers, residence, or other such expenses. These make up the bulk of the costs for many students.

Education Tax Credit

You are allowed a tax credit for every month or part-month you were enrolled in a qualifying post-secondary program during the year. Until recently, this credit was available only to full-time students, with the exception of disabled students, but that has changed (see Part-Time Students). The basic amount allowed for a full-time student has now been increased to $200 per month. If you were attending a regular university program, you would be eligible for a claim covering eight months. That total is then multiplied by 17 percent to determine the actual amount of the federal tax credit. In this case, it would work out to $272 ($1,600 x 17% = $272). Your provincial tax payable will also be reduced as a result of this credit. So the total value in terms of reducing taxes payable will be about $400, depending on your province of residence.

Carry-Forwards

The education and tuition credits can be used only to reduce your taxable income to zero. Once that has been achieved, you have two options if any credits remain. The first, which is quite new, is to carry forward the unused credits to future years and apply them as needed. However, be aware that if you decide to go this route, you will not be able to use the second option (described below) for any amount carried forward.

Transfers to Supporting Persons

The other choice for unused tuition and education credits is to transfer them to a supporting person. In most cases, this would be a parent, but it could also be a spouse. Before any amount can be transferred, however, the student must first reduce his or her taxable income to zero. There is a limit of $5,000 on the amount that can be transferred by any one student. For you to make the claim, the student must sign over form T2202A, which you will have to file with your return.

Moving Expenses

Students who move more than forty kilometres to attend college are technically eligible to claim moving costs. These may include travel expenses, the cost of shipping personal effects, and the like. But here's the catch: the expenses are deductible only from income earned at the new place of residence. For a student, this means he or she will have to receive scholarship money or perhaps a research grant of some type. But even if the child does get an academic grant, it may not be enough to put him or her into a taxable situation. So the deduction won't be of any use. Unfortunately, the parents, who are the ones who will probably actually pick up the tab in most cases, cannot claim these costs against their own income. This is just one more example of how the tax system places a burden on parents trying to help pay for their children's education. There is one angle that may apply down the road. If the student returns home (or goes to another city) to work at a summer job, moving costs are deductible against income from that source.

Scholarship Deduction
The first $500 in scholarship money is tax-free. This also covers fellowships, bursaries, study grants, and artists' project grants. If the total amount you receive from such sources is less than $500, it needn't be reported. If it is more than $500, subtract that amount and report only the balance on your tax return. For example, if you receive $3,000 in scholarship money, you need report only $2,500.

RRSP Education Withdrawals
The 1998 federal budget contained a new plan to allow Canadians to make withdrawals from an RRSP to further their education. Starting January 1, 1999, anyone enrolled in a full-time training or higher-education program for at least three months during the year can borrow up to $10,000 from their RRSP. These withdrawals may be spaced out for up to four years, but may not exceed $20,000 in total. The amount withdrawn must be repaid to the RRSP over a ten-year period, starting the last year after the person is enrolled full time (or six years after the first withdrawal, if that comes first). If any instalments are missed, the amount due will be added to the person's taxable income in that year. This program will be of only limited benefit, however, since most post-secondary students do not have any RRSP savings.

Student Loan Interest Tax Credit
Mounting student debt and the social and financial problems it is creating have forced the government to take steps to provide more relief in this area. The 1998 budget contained measures that will allow students to claim a 17 percent federal tax credit on the interest charges they pay for federal or provincial student loans. This could work out to be an important tax break, since the average student debt load is now about $25,000. If the interest rate is 8 percent, that works out to $2,000 a year. A federal credit on that amount would reduce tax payable by $340. With provincial taxes factored in, the total saving would be in the neighbourhood of $500.

Part-Time Students

In recent years, the government has been moving to provide more tax assistance to part-time students. In 1998, for the first time, part-timers were able to claim an education tax credit in the amount of $60. To be eligible, they had to be enrolled in a course that lasted at least three weeks and that included a minimum of twelve hours of course work per month. Also new for 1998 is a provision that allows part-time students to claim child-care expenses for the period they were enrolled in a qualifying program. Single parents may deduct the amount directly; in two-income families, the higher-income spouse may make the claim. Part-time students are also eligible for the tuition tax credit, providing the rules regarding length of course, etc., are met.

GST/HST Credit

Although this is not a student tax credit as such, many students miss out on it because they do not file a tax return. The GST/HST credit is available to anyone age nineteen or older who qualifies from an income perspective. This is a refundable credit, which means that if you don't owe enough tax against which to write it off, Ottawa will send you a cheque. Most college students qualify for it, but many don't receive it because you must file a tax return to make the claim.

Appendix 2

Adding Up the Costs

The price of a college education goes up every year. In an effort to keep track of the increases and provide up-to-date information on the costs, the USC Education Savings Plans organization surveys universities across Canada annually and publishes the results in a special brochure. They have been doing this for more than twenty years.

Not all universities participate, but enough (thirty in the most recent survey) do take part to offer a clear picture of current costs, historical patterns, and future projections.

The following data show the situation at the end of the 1997–98 academic year, based on information provided by the universities to USC. Our thanks to USC for allowing us to reproduce these figures here.

TABLE 1:
UNIVERSITY COSTS: ESTIMATED BREAKDOWN BY PROVINCE
(Excluding Local Travel and Other Expenses), 1997–98

Province and School	Tuition/ Fees	Room and Board	Books/ Supplies	Total Cost
Newfoundland				
Memorial University	$5,028	$5,846	$1,500	$12,374
Prince Edward Island				
University of PEI	3,507	5,500	1,500	10,507
Nova Scotia				
Acadia University	4,759	5,400	800	10,959
Dalhousie University	4,050	5,250	800	10,100
Mount Saint Vincent University	3,854	4,700	680	9,234
Saint Francis Xavier University	3,898	5,400	1,060	10,358
Saint Mary's University	3,844	5,200	1,000	10,044
Provincial Average	*4,081*	*5,190*	*868*	*10,139*
New Brunswick				
Université de Moncton	2,679	4,400	1,100	8,179
University of New Brunswick	3,359	4,300	900	8,559
St. Thomas University	2,741	3,800	600	7,141
Provincial Average	*2,926*	*4,167*	*867*	*7,960*
Quebec				
Bishop's University	2,910	3,718	900	7,528
Concordia University	2,884	1,856	1,200	5,940
Université du Québec à Montréal	1,870	3,200	700	5,770
McGill University	3,603	5,200	700	9,503
Provincial Average	*2,817*	*3,494*	*875*	*7,185*
Ontario				
Brock University	3,458	4,000	500	7,958
Carleton University	3,884	5,625	710	10,219
University of Guelph	3,699	5,000	710	9,409
McMaster University	3,684	5,600	735	10,019
Queen's University	3,816	5,789	700	10,305
University of Toronto	3,805	5,952	900	10,657
Trent University	3,897	5,571	780	10,248
Wilfrid Laurier University	3,689	5,500	735	9,924
York University	3,748	5,200	650	9,598
Provincial Average	*3,813*	*5,360*	*713*	*9,886*

TABLE 1: cont'd

Province and School	Tuition/ Fees	Room and Board	Books/ Supplies	Total Cost
Manitoba				
Brandon University	2,688	4,269	800	7,757
University of Manitoba	2,980	4,417	1,218	8,615
Provincial Average	*2,834*	*4,343*	*1,009*	*8,186*
Saskatchewan				
University of Saskatchewan	2,936	3,976	877	7,789
Alberta				
University of Alberta	3,455	4,377	800	8,632
University of Calgary	3,568	4,453	765	8,786
Provincial Average	*3,512*	*4,415*	*783*	*8,709*
British Columbia				
University of British Columbia	2,648	5,260	570	8,478
University of Victoria	2,554	5,400	858	8,812
Provincial Average	*2,601*	*5,330*	*714*	*8,645*

Figures supplied by participating universities. Where a range of costs were provided, average or typical costs were used.

TABLE 2:
NATIONAL AVERAGE FOR UNIVERSITY COSTS

	With Residence	Without Residence
National Average University Cost 1997–98	$10,615	$5,919
Average Increase over 1996–97	0%	9.20%
Average Annual Rate of Increase 1975–97	6.60%	7.40%

TABLE 3:
FUTURE UNIVERSITY COST PROJECTIONS

Academic Year of Admission to Studies	*Cost of Four-Year Program (With Residence)*	*Cost of Four-Year Program (Without Residence)*
2003–04	$68,700	$40,600
2004–05	73,300	43,600
2005–06	78,100	46,800
2006–07	83,300	50,300
2007–08	88,800	54,000
2008–09	94,600	58,000
2009–10	100,900	62,300
2010–11	107,500	66,900
2011–12	114,600	71,800
2012–13	122,200	77,100
2013–14	130,300	82,800
2014–15	138,900	89,000
2015–16	148,000	95,600

Index